ecoo

landscapes & masterplans by ha

Leon van Schaik

WILEY-ACADEMY

ecocells

Published in Great Britain in 2003 by Wiley-Academy, a division of John Wiley & Sons Ltd

Copyright © 2003

John Wiley & Sons Ltd, The Atrium, Southern Gate, Chichester, West Sussex PO19 8SQ, England
Telephone (+44) 1243 779777

Email (for orders and customer service enquiries): cs-books@wiley.co.uk
Visit our Home Page on www.wileyeurope.com or www.wiley.com

ADF Management Sdn Bhd
8, Jalan 1, Taman Sri Ukay, Off Jalan Ulu Klang,
68000 Ampang, Selangor, Malaysia
Telephone (+603) 4257 1966

All Rights Reserved. No part of this publication may be reproduced, stored in a retrieval system or transmitted in any form or any means, electronic, mechanical, photocopying, recording, scanning or otherwise, except under the terms of the Copyright, Designs and Patents Act 1988 or under the terms of a licence issued by the Copyright Licensing Agency Ltd, 90 Tottenham Court Road, London W1T 4LP, UK, without the permissions in writing of the Publisher. Requests to the Publisher should be addressed to the Permissions Department, John Wiley & Sons Ltd, The Atrium, Southern Gate, Chichester, West Sussex PO19 8SQ, England, or emailed to permreq@wiley.co.uk, or faxed to (+44) 1243 770571.

ISBN 0-470-85119-8

Design by Kenneth Cheong
Printed and bound in Malaysia by EHT Creative & Graphic Services
for Asia Design Forum Publications

Contents

1. Simultaneity by Leon van Schaik   5

2. West Kowloon Waterfront Urban Ecosystem   11

3. FNWI Development, University of Amsterdam Urban Ecosystem   79

4. Design as Eco-mimesis by Ken Yeang   137

1. Simultaneity
by Leon Van Schaik

Contradiction and Complexity in Architecture, Venturi's mid-century sound-bite, punctured the ideology of 'form follows function' and opened Architecture to the surreal by presenting a critical landscape, long described by Salvador Dali - both the perpetrator and the victim of an imagined terrain. Dali is the emblematic figure of the mid-century because his work seeks to reconcile the glory and the horror of human achievement that writhe through the history of the time at personal and societal scale. In a simulacrum to Einstein's theory of relativity, or perhaps more acutely to the paradox of quantum theory in which matter is and simultaneously is not, Dali's imagined world contorts to allow the irreconcilable to coexist. This is his genius. The double-bind that ties him to this liminal territory as a victim was a passion deeply felt but culturally inexpressible, given the machismo of the mental world of the Latin male. In a duality that he spent a life-time denying, the artist – in love with a soul-mate who happened to be of the same gender – scribbled doggerel while the object of his adoration, the poet Lorca, drew copiously a world

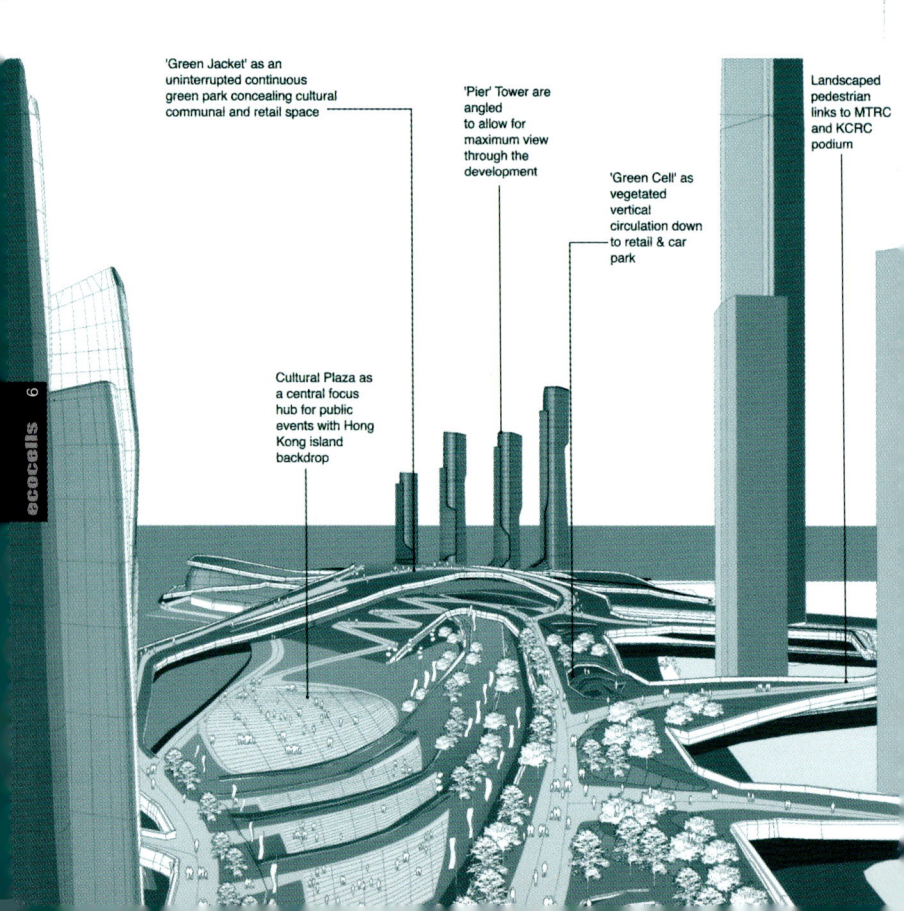

'Green Jacket' as an uninterrupted continuous green park concealing cultural communal and retail space

'Pier' Tower are angled to allow for maximum view through the development

'Green Cell' as vegetated vertical circulation down to retail & car park

Landscaped pedestrian links to MTRC and KCRC podium

Cultural Plaza as a central focus hub for public events with Hong Kong island backdrop of unlikely combinations. On the beaches of a summer that both energised and tormented their future lives, they drew profiles of the one that cast the shadow of the other. So innocent and total that they allowed photographs of them wearing the same suit, one in the pants, the other in the jacket. Stung by their peers' mocking of the intensity of their identification with each other, this couple drew apart, working through their lives to recreate a testimony in their own mediums to the fixations of happiness that a summer on a beach without social constraint had gifted them. In retrospect the ultra right political tide that then engulfed their lives forged them as artists of the tragedy that is the new condition of the twenty-first century: simultaneity. Architecture is a latecomer to this mental landscape. Utilitarian preoccupations of re-construction delayed analysis of the central paradox of the destructive force of what we create. Even today the major mode of construction is dimly resonant of the styles of modernism predicated on industrial sheds, ships and aeroplanes, or of classicism as an applique external decoration. Only one architect has made it his major project to attempt to reconcile the irresistible drives of economic 'growth'. Oh! How we love to death. How we see a beautiful hill, seek to own it and build a house on it! How we see a lovely boulevard and decide to build our corporate HQ there, just there! From his apprenticeship under Archigram, Yeang sought through his doctorate the proper tools for achieving their dreams of moving, responsive, self-mending cities.

No other architect of our era engages so fully with the condition of simultaneity as Ken Yeang, manifested in the work of his firm of Hamzah & Yeang (® T. R. Hamzah & Yeang Sdn. Bhd.) with his business partner, Tengku Robert Hamzah. Here the colonial boy, growing up in an Osbert Lancaster modern house in provincial Penang, is given access by imperial accident to the highlights of London in the 1960s. An extra on the set of Antonioni's "Blow Up", a black clad dandy in London's 20th century heyday, Yeang is suddenly both province and metropolis personified. Riding on this parabola, he does not succumb to the blandishments of the establishment in either sphere, but commences on a career of both and that is the exemplar of what Dali and Lorca might have been had they not succumbed to the tragic, the one choosing denial and the other failing to escape to the New World.

Yeang's career is an attempt at reconciliation of opposites. Over and again he mixes mercury and water. His tropical verandah city sought to preserve the pleasures of the colonial town within the rampant development of the post-colonial era. When developers rushed headlong into Manhattan mode, Yeang attempted to subvert their flight from the horizontal into bio-climatically designed eco-towers. He used his science to co-opt the vertical into the same daydream of the healthy social organism of the prosperous town. In Yeang's designs, chains of green and leafy places in which people can meet, conjugate and converse, snake their way up the sides of skyscrapers that flap open and shut as they seek to engage people in the airs and vapours of a soft tropical night. As soon as the opportunity presents itself – a plan for re-vitalising the old city of Taipei – Yeang up-ends the tower and creates the 'ground-scraper', two later versions of which, one in Kowloon, the other in Amsterdam, form this exhibit. In his sky-scrapers, what were verandahs became sky-courts. On their side these become fissures and canyons into a new, forest-covered, artificial ground, allowing light, air and plant growth deep inside the developments. The architect calls these "ecocells".

The "ecocell" is a concept they have developed as a means of integrating the inorganic mass of the built components with the organic landscaping. In essence it is a cell-like void that is cut into the building and slicing down through all floors from the uppermost to the basement. "Ecocells" are located at regular intervals in the building. Each "ecocell" serves several functions: it brings daylight and natural ventilation into the inner parts of the building. it has a ramp that brings the vegetation from the roof down to all floors and to the basement. At the base of each "ecocell" are the algae sewerage treatment water tanks that convert sewerage waste into pure water. Why the town? Remember that without the town there is no citizen, and without the civil-being there is no civilisation. In towns there is food, fashion, art and discourse between the generations and the classes. In the realm of city-making, Yeang is the magician who morphs any development proposal into Prospero's magic isle: be it tall, squat, fat, thin or long, there is a way to engage it in the daydream of ease on a verandah that holds childhood 'motionless in its arms.' So it is that this almost always flying architect constantly recreates serene moments from a childhood in the tropics. So it is that this architect combines analytical discourse conveyed in graphs and pie charts with the magic of stolen, half forgotten moments that subliminally connect his hard-bitten, financially-macho clients back to the timelessness of their youth. Reminds them after all of what it is that matters about being alive. Some clusters of towers are indeed simple extrusions of necessity. Yeang however takes us into a romance of being. Here he is providing the allure of unencumbered engagement with the world that his tutor, Archigram promised, but he promotes it through the facts, not the form. So where the Archigram Monte Carlo Casino proposal is merely underground, Yeang's ground-scrapers are riven with holes that pull light deep into their recesses. He constructs a new nature preoccupied with our need to experience the wilderness that we are loving-to-death. If through these designs we inhabit steep valleys and caverns, then we may be able to retreat from the country and allow it to be repaired.

In these new ground-scrapers, we are invited to live within an artificial ground plane, reminiscent of the re-engineering of Chicago in the 19th century, but not simply utilitarian as then. Then water carried canal barges, and was turned around to make the canals connect to the docks. False ground was created to separate services from pedestrians and privileged vehicular access. In the ground-scrapers, buildings do create false ground, but on this earth shield sits a new landscape, a tropical or temperate jungle matted over and hanging into the breathing and lighting holes of layer upon layer of human intercourse/concourse.

Study these proposals carefully. Their conception is clearly diagrammed. It can seem matter-of-fact. The designs assume however a world in which life is a zestful chain of meetings in bars and cafes, a world of flaneur-ship and flirtation, of sheer joy of human connection and folly. A world of newness, of fast service, quick new ways of producing images, of young ideas of design and new faces on old friends. From an architect who knows the best place for a repro service in Tokyo, Singapore, Sydney or London. Who avidly spots new talent amongst designers and artists wherever he goes. A man who nurtures friendships in cities all around the globe. As if they all were in one verandah-city and his peregrinations are simply his evening promenade. The architect models the globally distributed town by knowing where all the best places are in every city. This year's, not last year's places. He checks the pulse of the world, and invites everyone to do the same but only more so in an improbable simultaneity of consumption and sustainability. The gondola prows of the combed up slabs and towers rise out of the artificial forests and reveal the imperative of the dollar, but they all tie back to what can be given in return to the crust of the earth. A few metres of soil, a fringe of foliage. New subterranean flows. Light and breeze and human contemplation, folly and humour and entrepreneurial wizardry.

Leon van Schaik

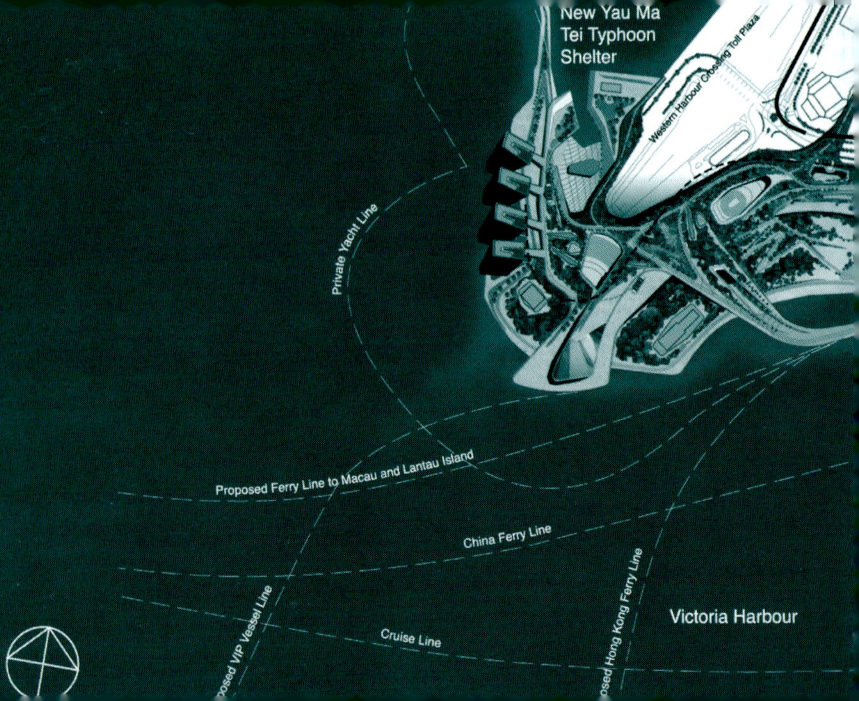

ecocells 10

New Yau Ma Tei Typhoon Shelter

Western Harbour Crossing Toll Plaza

Private Yacht Line

Proposed Ferry Line to Macau and Lantau Island

China Ferry Line

Proposed VIP Vessel Line

Cruise Line

Proposed Hong Kong Ferry Line

Victoria Harbour

2. West Kowloon Waterfront Urban Ecosystem

- Airport Railway/Kowloon Station
- KCRC's West Rail West Kowloon Station
- Possible new location for Fire Station, ie 'Station in the Park'
- Ecological Corridor to extend into Kowloon Park
- Internal Rapid Transit System (IRTS) to connect to Tsim Sha Tsui MTR station
- Ocean Terminal
- Kowloon Park
- Tsim Sha Tsui

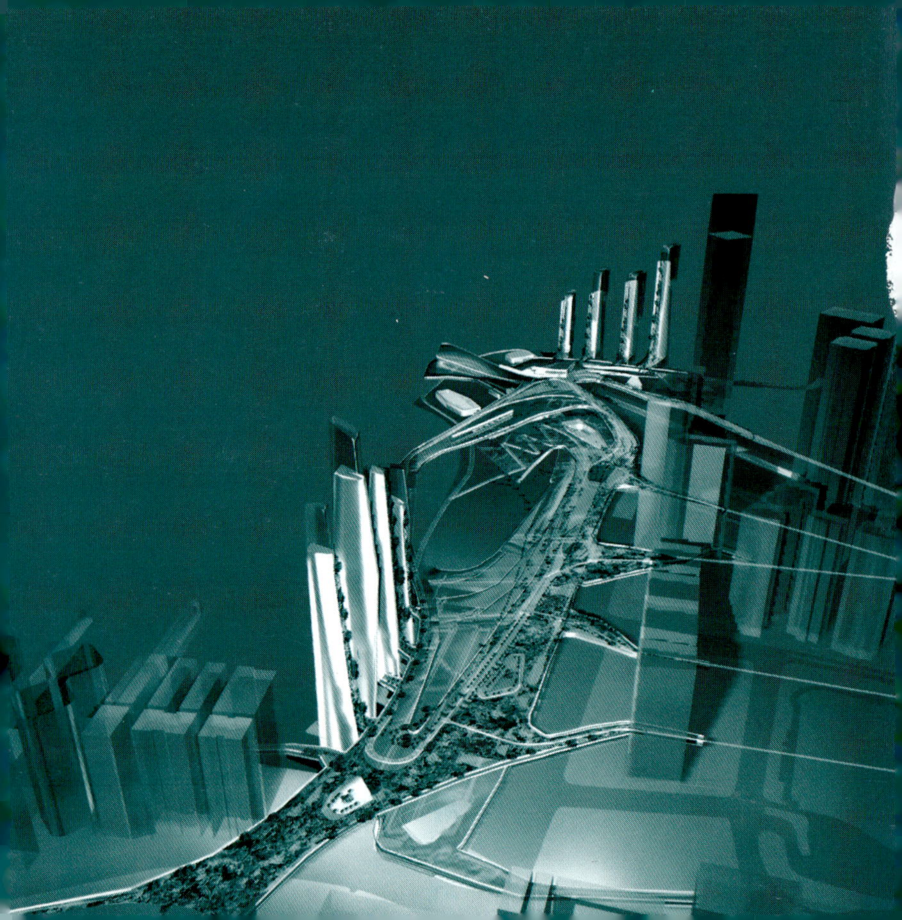

The Ecological Corridor

This site provides the last opportunity to give to Hong Kong a great urban park equivalent to those found in major cities of the world like Central Park in New Park or Hyde Park in London.

With a new landscaped site-coverage of over 94%, this will be the largest urban park in Hong Kong, framing the waterfront in a lush green dynamic setting. Our masterplan focuses on the park as an "ecological corridor" that links key green spaces in Kowloon, as a "necklace" that links together waterfront activities, commercial, retail, residential, cultural and recreational community spaces in one single unique development.

Perspective of the new West Kowloon Waterfront development from Victoria Peak

This "ecological corridor" is designed as a "green jacket" over the retail, entertainment, cultural and other facilities that are placed on top, below, or sandwiched between the green jacket. "Ecocells" are introduced to bring natural light, natural ventilation and pedestrians from the park down to the subterranean parking.

This is an ecological design solution that seeks to provide an environmentally sustainable urban ecosystem as a major park within the intensive city of Hong Kong, while fulfilling the arts, cultural and recreational programmes of the community.

This is the landscaped-roof level. The roof is planted with dense vegetation to provide a buffer against Austin Road and forms an ecological corridor as a lush backdrop to the built-form.

An outdoor amphitheatre follows the slope of the landscape, mounding with views towards the harbour as a stage backdrop. This becomes the new "Peak", a prime vantage viewing point and public space, accessed by pedestrian and cycle paths that weave throughout this level, integrating with the rest of the site.

- 60 Storey Apartment
- 45 Storey Apartment
- 45 Storey Apartment
- 30 Storey Apartment
- Marina with outdoor cafes, restaurant
- Fishing Museum
- Louvred Glass Roof over Retail
- Western Harbour Crossing
- Louvred Glass Roof over Retail
- Yacht Docking Quay for Apartment Residents
- Louvred Roof over Ventilation Building
- Opera House
- Outdoor Amphitheater
- Louvred Glass Roof over Retail
- Louvred Roof over Ventilation Building

Residential | Arts & Culture

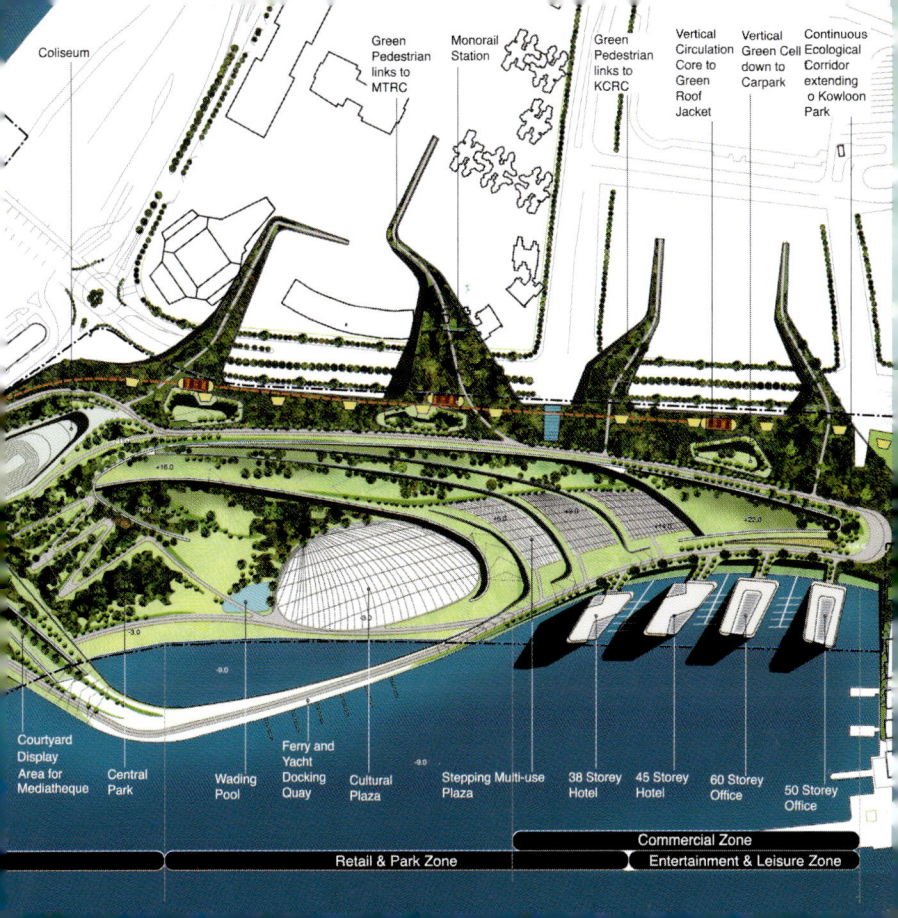

- Coliseum
- Green Pedestrian links to MTRC
- Monorail Station
- Green Pedestrian links to KCRC
- Vertical Circulation Core to Green Roof Jacket
- Vertical Green Cell down to Carpark
- Continuous Ecological Corridor extending to Kowloon Park

- Courtyard Display Area for Mediatheque
- Central Park
- Wading Pool
- Ferry and Yacht Docking Quay
- Cultural Plaza
- Stepping Multi-use Plaza
- 38 Storey Hotel
- 45 Storey Hotel
- 60 Storey Office
- 50 Storey Office

Retail & Park Zone

Commercial Zone

Entertainment & Leisure Zone

This is the 1st level consisting of a shopping mall on the northern edge that extends east to west along Austin Road, transforming the street into an active shopping boulevard. The shopping mall is sufficiently set back from the road to allow for a service road with waiting zones and queuing lanes.

The vehicular traffic road enters the site at this level and ramps down to Level B1 (to avoid crossing pedestrian routes to the waterfront park). The road onto Level 1 toward the west as it leads to the Opera House and waterfront residential development, giving a dramatic effect as the drivers emerge to a stunning view of Hong Kong island.

The new waterfront will be punctuated by forms that extend into the coast line; the pier tower groupings on the east and west extremes, the opera house, the 'jewel' that grows out from the land into the water, and a mediatheque that blends with the landscape. A main waterfront plaza on this level provides for outdoor cultural activities to take place.

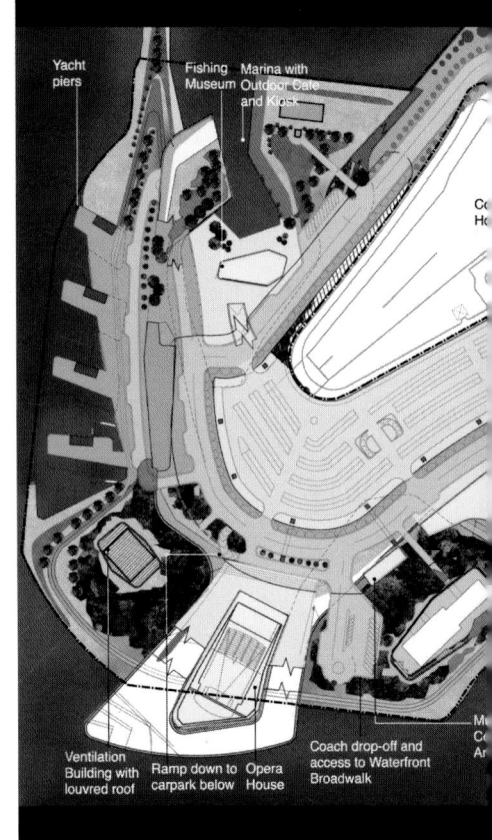

Yacht piers
Fishing Museum
Marina with Outdoor Cafe and Kiosk
Ventilation Building with louvred roof
Ramp down to carpark below
Opera House
Coach drop-off and access to Waterfront Broadwalk

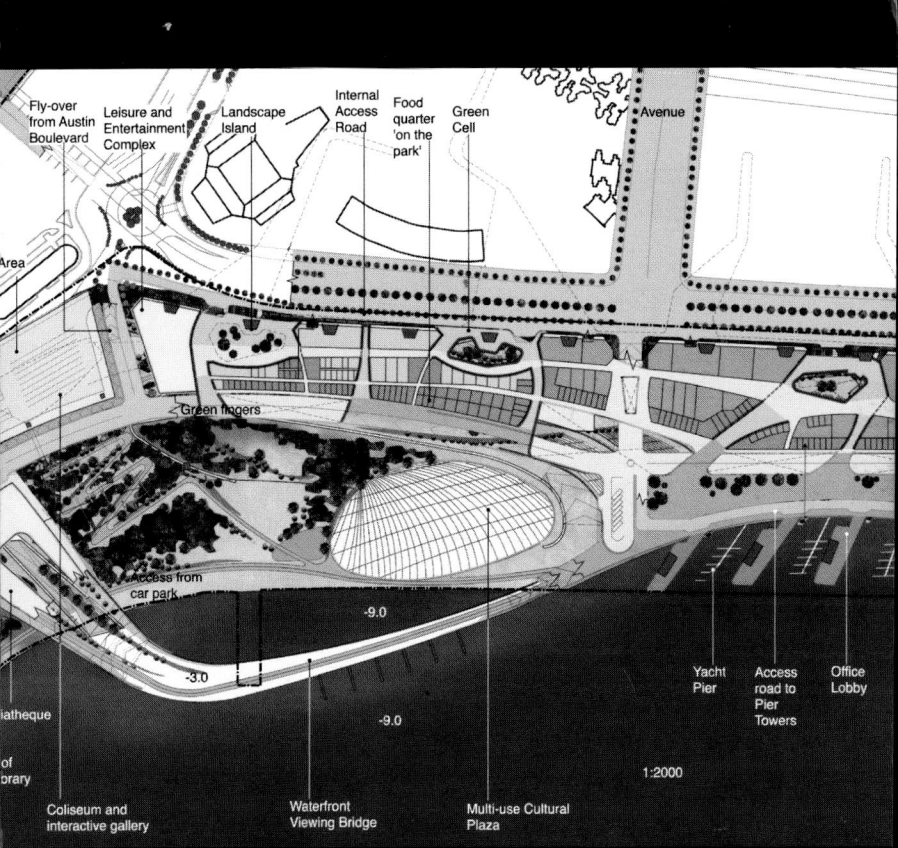

Fly-over from Austin Boulevard | Leisure and Entertainment Complex | Landscape Island | Internal Access Road | Food quarter 'on the park' | Green Cell | Avenue

Area

Green fingers

Access from car park

−3.0

−9.0

−9.0

iathèque

of brary

Coliseum and interactive gallery | Waterfront Viewing Bridge | Multi-use Cultural Plaza | Yacht Pier | Access road to Pier Towers | Office Lobby

1:2000

This is the 2nd level of the shopping mall, and the entry level to the coliseum. The south facade of the shopping mall is stepped back, creating outdoor landscaped terraces for leisure spaces (e.g. cafes, dining) with views towards the harbour.

The coliseum has an expansive sheltered forecourt under the green roof jacket which could also be a spill-over space for concerts with views towards Victoria Harbour. An internal rapid transit system (monorail) provides east-west connection across the development and beyond to Kowloon Park and Tsim Sha Tsui.

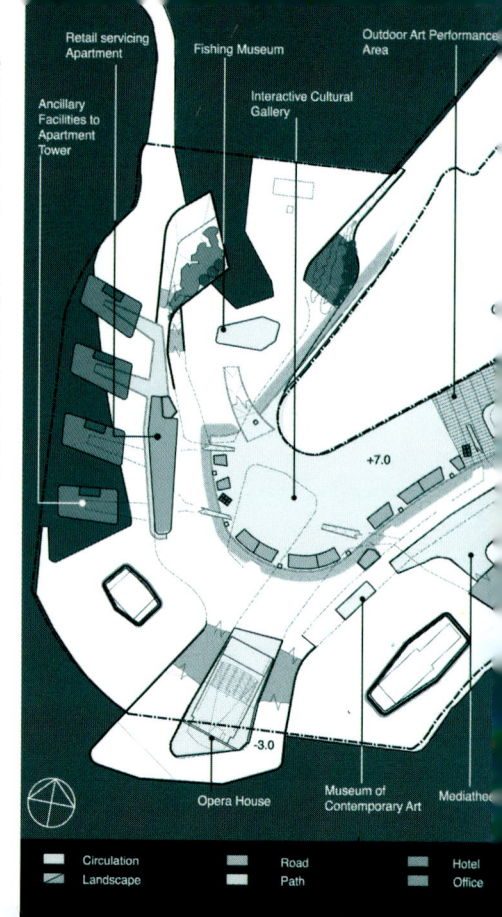

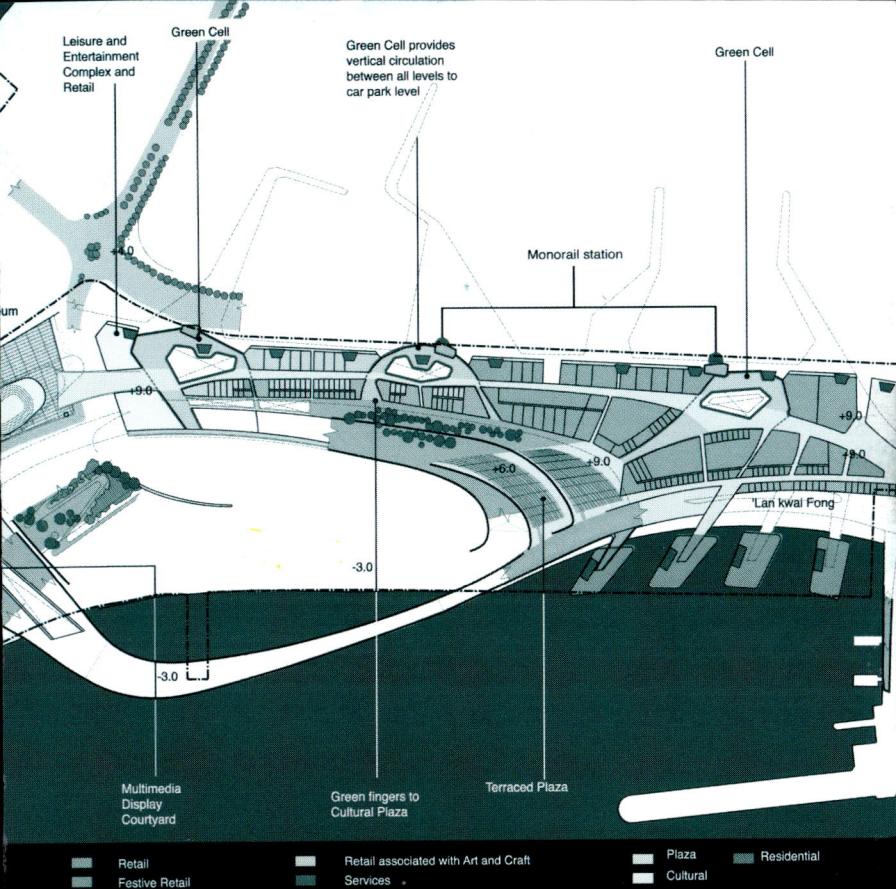

- Leisure and Entertainment Complex and Retail
- Green Cell
- Green Cell provides vertical circulation between all levels to car park level
- Green Cell
- Monorail station
- 'Lan kwai Fong'
- Multimedia Display Courtyard
- Green fingers to Cultural Plaza
- Terraced Plaza

+4.0
+9.0
+9.0
+6.0
-9.0
-3.0
-3.0

Retail	Retail associated with Art and Craft	Plaza — Residential
Festive Retail	Services	Cultural

A continuous waterfront promenade stretches from the Tsim Sha Tsui's Ferry Terminals on the east of the site to the new proposed residential development on the north-west, as a public recreational space. The waterfront view of the development will be characterised by more lush greenery that terraces up from level B1 to the podium roof.

A viewing bridge extends out to the harbour doubling up as a boat docking area. The jetty also acts as a wave breaker, sheltering a calmer body of water adjacent to the green park.

The car parking is located on level B1 and concealed by thick vegetation and the earth mounding up to Level 1.

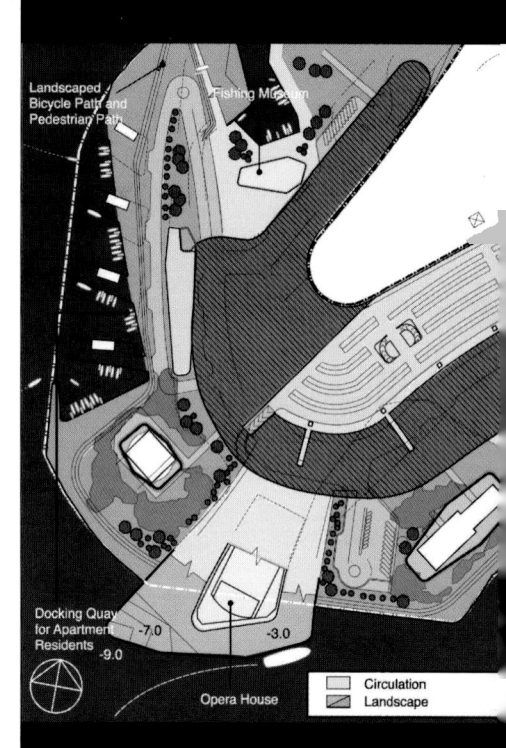

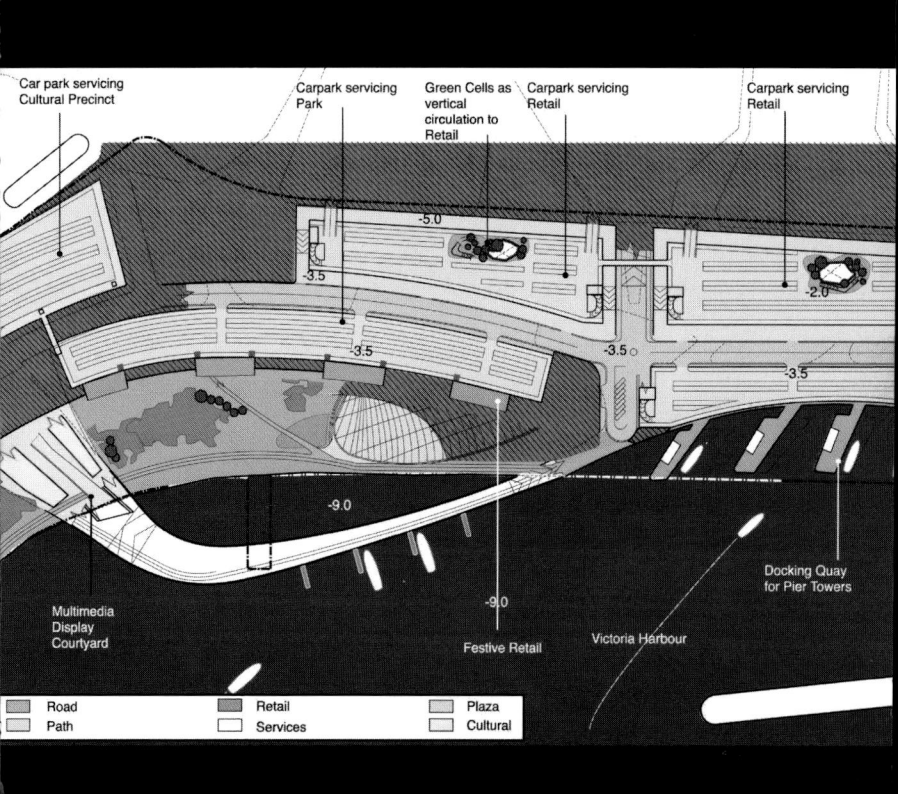

Car park servicing Cultural Precinct	
Carpark servicing Park	
Green Cells as vertical circulation to Retail	
Carpark servicing Retail	
Carpark servicing Retail	
Multimedia Display Courtyard	
Festive Retail	
Docking Quay for Pier Towers	
Victoria Harbour	

Legend:
- Road
- Path
- Retail
- Services
- Plaza
- Cultural

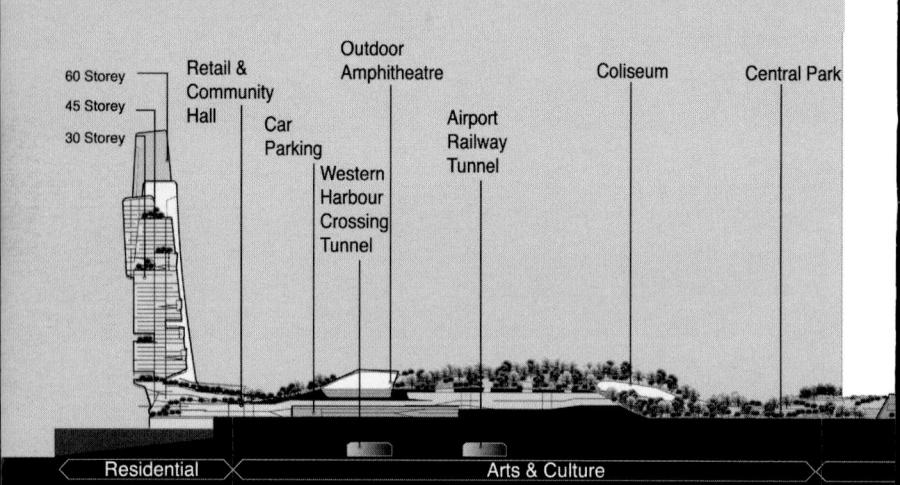

60 Storey	Retail & Community Hall		Outdoor Amphitheatre		Coliseum	Central Park
45 Storey		Car Parking		Airport Railway Tunnel		
30 Storey			Western Harbour Crossing Tunnel			

Residential | Arts & Culture

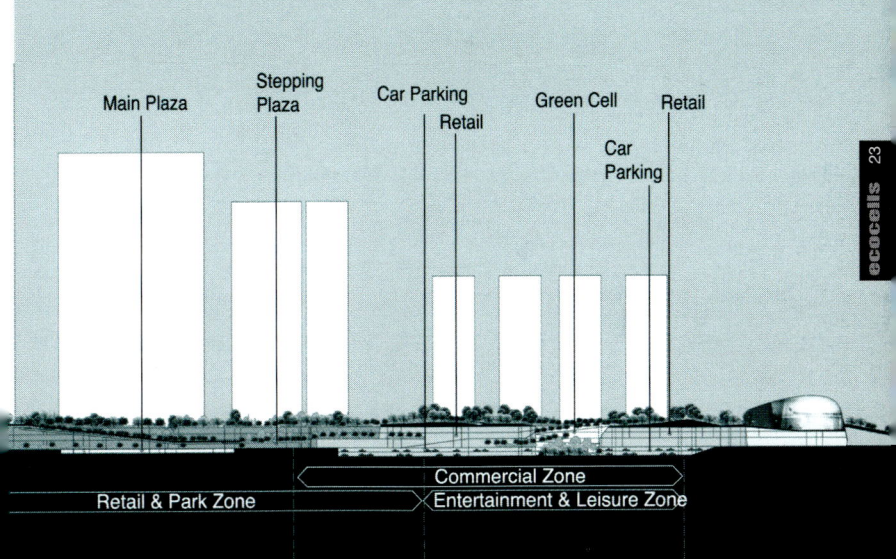

North-South section across the site and the property at the north of the site

Opera House

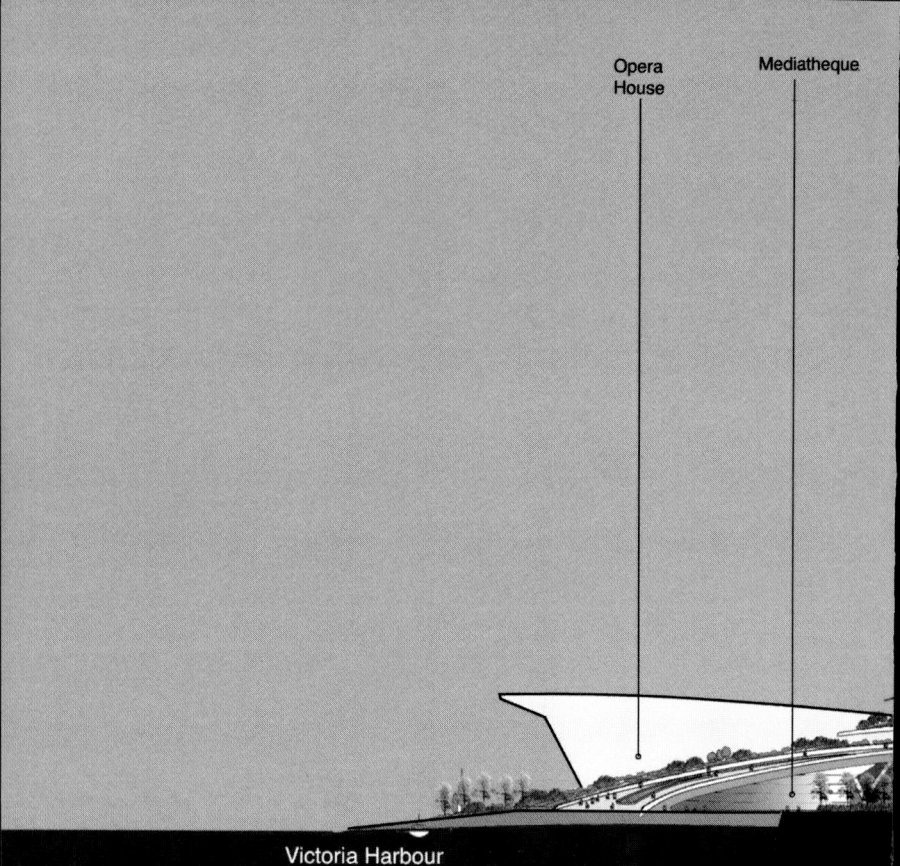

Mediatheque

Victoria Harbour

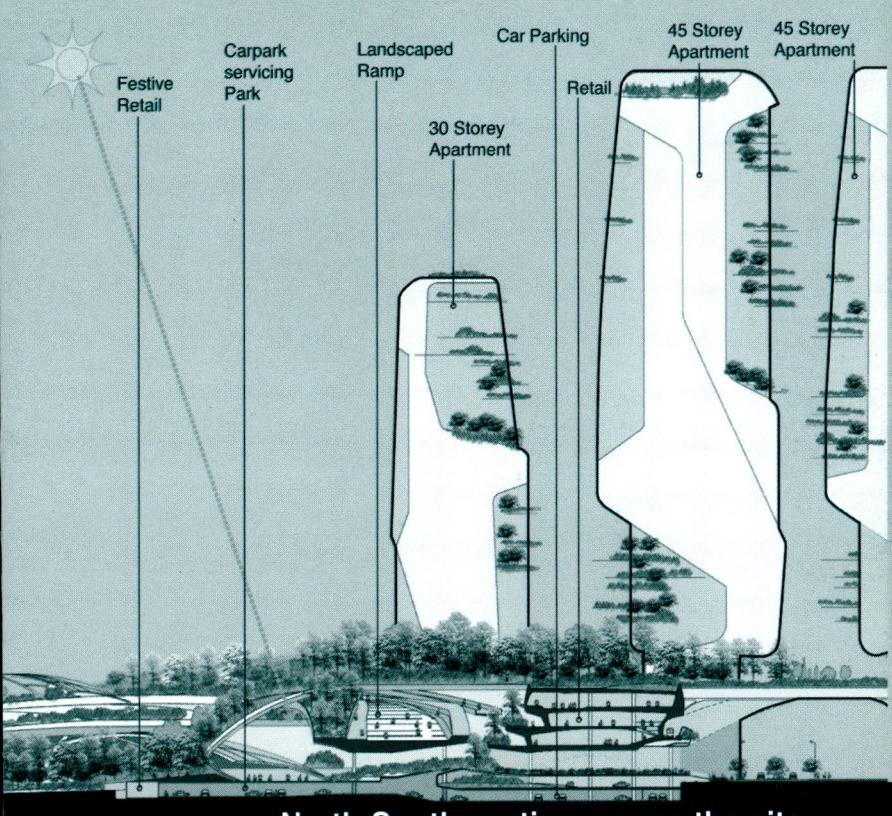

North-South section across the site showing Waterfront

Opera House becomes a light beacon along Waterfront

uninterrupted views of Hong Kong island from KCRC and MTRC Tower are maintained

- Waterfront Promenade extend into Waterfront
- Cultural Plaza with visual links to Hong Kong Island
- Pier Towers angled to minimise obstruction of view towards Victoria Harbour from Kowloon Island

Contextually the site is at the tip of a complex and richly dense peninsular facing a dynamic city island. Meeting and enhancing the demands of the city of Hong Kong has brought about in the scheme a continuous "green jacket" that encapsulates and incorporates urban and natural elements of the Special Administrative Region of Hong Kong, from the forested hills to its urban canyons.

The "green jacket" formed by the landscaped park integrates the built forms between the ecological corridor, the cultural necklace of event spaces and the Waterfront Viewing bridge.

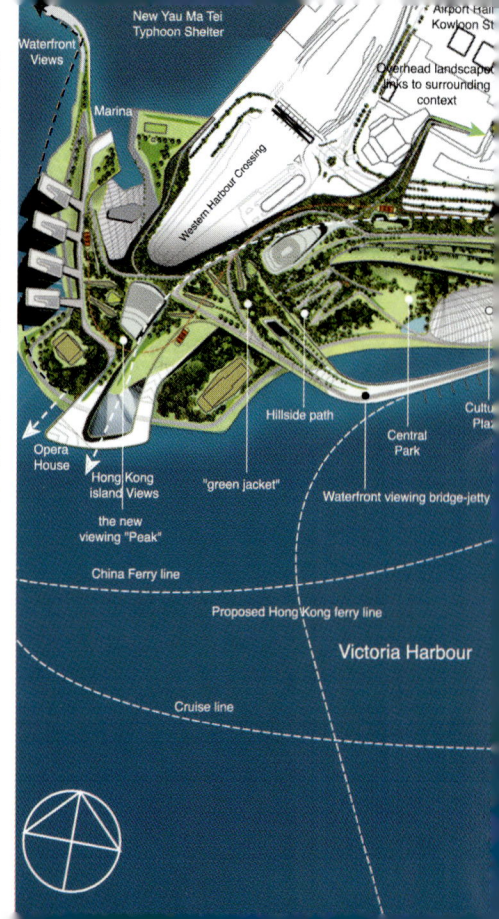

- "Ecological corridor"
- KCRC's West Rail West Kowloon Station
- Overhead landscaped links to surrounding context
- Lin Cheung Road
- Ecological corridor to extend into Kowloon Park
- Hong Kong island Views
- Link to Kowloon Park
- Internal Rapid Transit System (IRTS) to connect to Tsim Sha Tsui MTR station
- Ocean Terminal
- Hong Kong ferry line

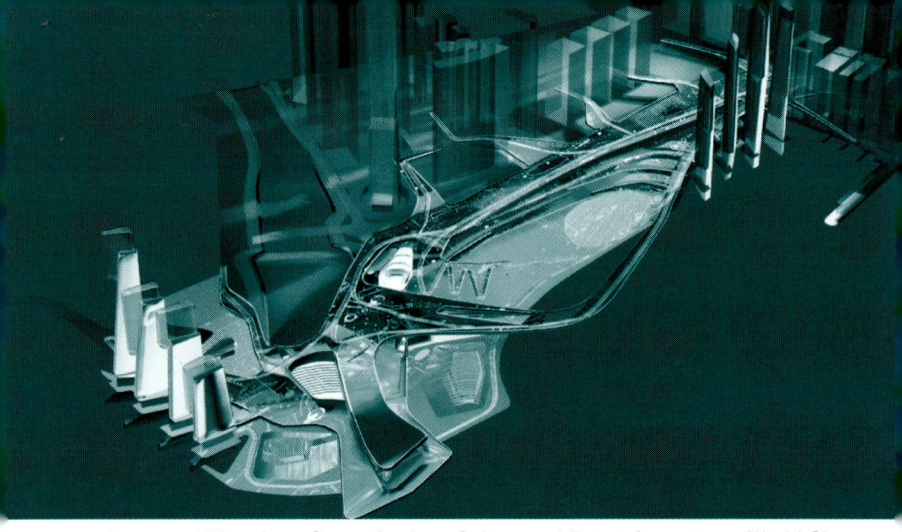

Integrated Waterfront Centre for Arts, Culture and Entertainment as a World-Class Destination

The wide range of recreational, cultural and retail integrated facilities will become a regional hub for users and tourists and is easily accessed through public transport, as well as ample coach parking.

Uninterrupted Views

MTRC and KCRC Towers maintain uninterrupted views of the waterfront through landscaped park. Within our proposal, vantage viewing areas are oriented to capture dramatic views of the waterfront and Hong Kong Island.

The Park as a "Green Jacket"

The landscaped roof provides a continuous urban "ecological corridor" and provides an environmentally-sustainable and ecologically benign solution. 94% of the site is covered by landscape park and vegetation.

Ecocells
These are located at critical locations along the "Green Jacket" to provide ventilation and natural lighting to the programmatic spaces as well as integrating existing transportation systems with new proposed networks.

Public Park spaces
The continuous extent of the "green jacket" roof offers many oppurtunities for active and passive public spaces through the landscape and urban interfaces, such as the Cultural Plaza.

Feng Shui
Consideration of Feng Shui design principles for auspicious conditions ensures a successful development.

Landscaped Urban Connections
The continuous landscaped park provides circulation within the site and overhead landscaped bridges connect with the surrounding context to form an integrated urban environment.

Integrated Cultural "necklace" of event spaces
Integrating the cultural loop of facilities such as the landmark Opera House, Cultural Plaza, Amphitheatre, Mediatheque and the retail district to the surrounding context will maximise user access.

Continuous Waterfront Promenade
The long stretch of the waterfront is to be optimised as a continuous promenade with enhanced facilities such as a Viewing Bridge, Marina and amenities while linking back to the existing waterfront pathway.

"Pier" Towers
The dynamics between the new landscaped form and marine environment is encapsulated in the pier towers. The towers are strategically located right on Victoria Harbour as well as forming a continuous green link from Central Park with vertical landscaping to the upper levels.

ecocells 32

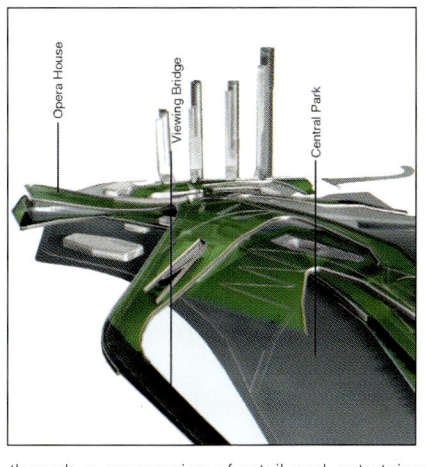

The design will benefit the surrounding context, local residents and the city of Hong Kong itself in several ways:

Integrating the arts, culture and entertainment precinct in Hong Kong
Arts and culturally-integrated facilities include: the Opera House, Mediatheque, Waterfront Museum, Open-air Amphitheatre, Sculpture Garden, Cultural Plaza and Coliseum - all blended into the multi-layered landscape park. Entertainment and recreational facilities include: an IMAX theatre, Cinema Multiplex, Coliseum, Viewing areas to Hong Kong and Active Park areas.

These facilities draw people up from the main shopping area of Tsim Sha Tsui through a progression of retail and entertainment spaces to the cultural heart of the scheme. These are all integrated by a continuous "cultural circulation-loop" that moves between each end of the site.

Creating a new iconic identity for Kowloon's waterfront
The design creates an entirely new landscaped waterfront feature for Hong Kong. New building typologies appropriate to the waterfront (e.g. "pier towers") directly address the harbour and the new Viewing Bridge enhances the waterfront promenade. A dedicated marine centre is also proposed, with a Marina for small boats, fishing jetty and a History of Fishing Museum. The proposal also emphasises the natural aspects of the site through connections between land (terrestrial ecosystems) and sea (aquatic ecosystems).

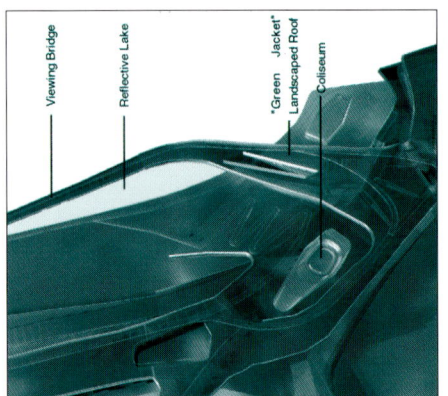

Image labels: Viewing Bridge; Reflective Lake; "Green Jacket" Landscaped Roof; Coliseum

Enhancing significantly the city's tourism potential

The new integrated arts and culture district can become a unique world-class tourist destination that combines and synthesises the landscape with the built form. It will serve the needs of the residents and visitors to Hong Kong in addition to becoming a prominent ecological and cultural symbol of Hong Kong.

Through the integration of the cultural areas with the retail complex and scenic promenades, this proposal enables a complex mix of spaces to draw users to circulate within and around the development. There will be key viewing areas on the landscaped roof and terraces, especially at the "peak" of the roof; the terraced park and the Waterfront Promenade, which are strategically positioned to capture prime vistas of Hong Kong. This is a relevant part of the experience of Hong Kong city, especially during festive occasions such as Dragon Boat Races and fireworks displays on special days.

Integrating the urban fabric and landscape for the locality

The emphasis is on an urban-design approach of providing physical links to the surrounding developments through overhead landscaped bridges. These urban connections include new communal activities linkages, overhead retail linkages to surrounding developments (e.g. MTRC), the "ecological corridor" links existing surrounding green areas (e.g. Kowloon Park), as a continuation of the waterfront promenade with provisions for future connections to other developments in the Yau Ma Tei area.

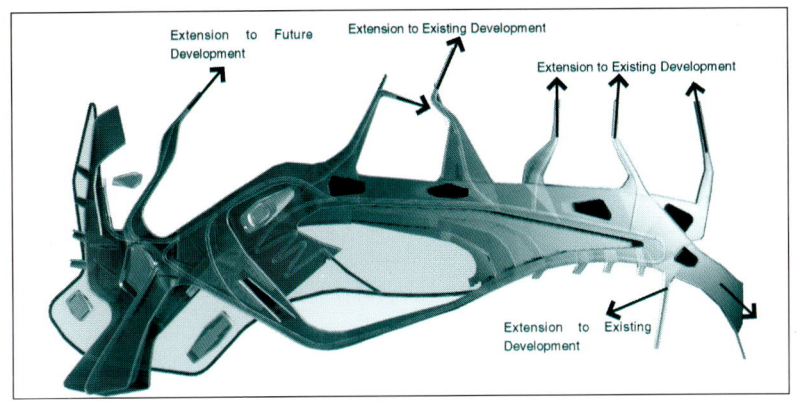

The design links the activities within the site to the surrounding areas of Kowloon, to provide a seamless integration from street level upwards. This is achieved through a series of landscaped overhead bridges and ramps that connect to street level and will direct users into the development. Continuity of the urban fabric is also provided through the continuous waterfront promenade to the commercial areas at the south of the site and pedestrian connections with Kowloon Park at the landscaped podium-level.

Optimising the site's maximum physical and commercial potential
Using the existing zoning as a baseline, the commercial content optimises the development of this site. The total commercial gross area is 528,400 sqm, with a net saleable area of 396,300 sqm 1,600 apartments are also included with a total gross area of 144,000 sqm.

Providing an adaptable urban design solution that allows for future needs
The design concept is sufficiently flexible to allow for future change, by varying the options of building phasing and opportunities for future regeneration (where required).

Detail of "ecolles"

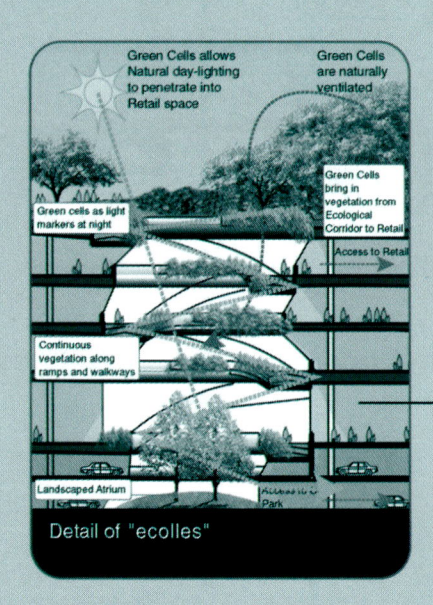

Victoria Harbour

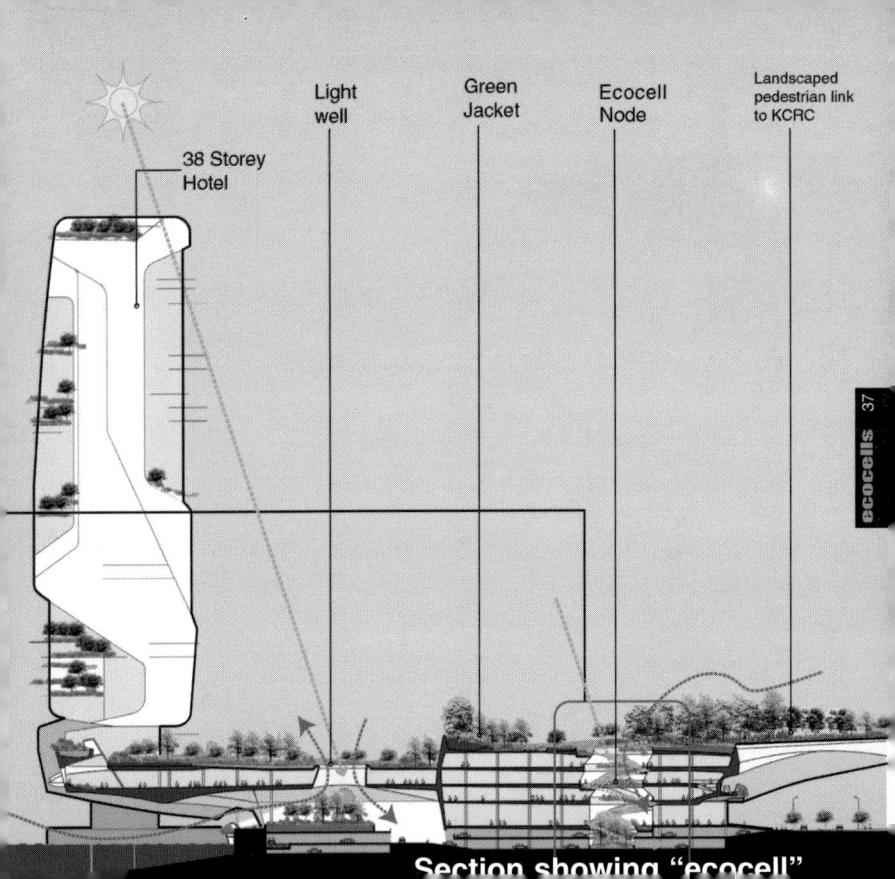

- 38 Storey Hotel
- Light well
- Green Jacket
- Ecocell Node
- Landscaped pedestrian link to KCRC

ecocells 37

Section showing "ecocell"

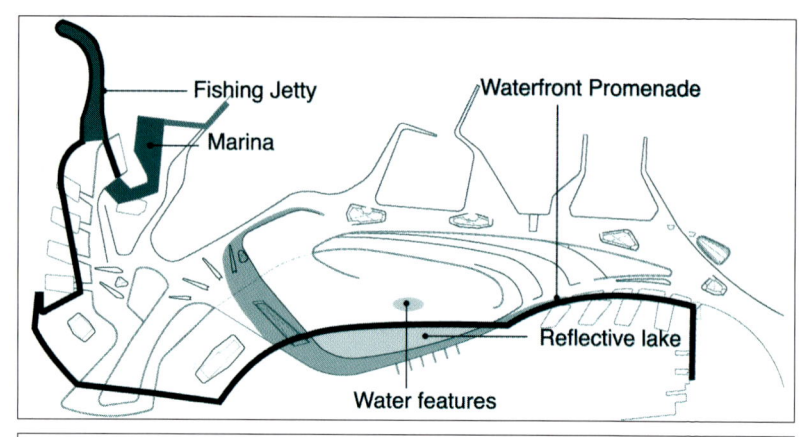

Top diagram labels
- Fishing Jetty
- Marina
- Waterfront Promenade
- Reflective lake
- Water features

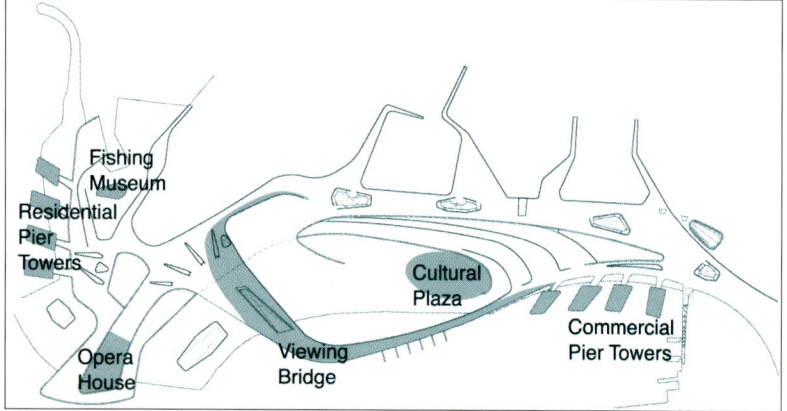

Bottom diagram labels
- Fishing Museum
- Residential Pier Towers
- Opera House
- Viewing Bridge
- Cultural Plaza
- Commercial Pier Towers

ecocells 38

The proposal creates an entirely new landscaped and active feature for the Kowloon waterfront. The design also emphasises the natural aspects of the site through connections between land (terrestrial ecosystems) and sea (aquatic ecosystems) and at the same time integrating cultural and community needs and commercial aspects.

Marine Features

A continuous Waterfront Promenade extends from the Marine Centre, the Opera House and the Viewing Bridge to the Waterfront Pier Towers at the edges of the site.

The Waterfront Promenade brings users on a scenic walk that captures and celebrates views of Hong Kong Harbour and the Island.

The Viewing Bridge provides a dramatic extension of the "green jacket" into Victoria Harbour, acting as a wave break to create a new lagoon in the Central Park. The extension forms a prime vantage viewing point towards the park and Hong Kong Island.

Access to boat docking is provided through jetties and ramps down to the Harbour, where the built form of the proposal comes into contact with the waterfront at the Viewing Bridge. Additional boat access is provided at the pier towers and Opera House for VIPs.

The Marina forms the culmination of the Waterfront Promenade at the far west end of the site. This marine area will include a fishing jetty, History of Fishing Museum as a showcase of Hong Kong's fishing history, local yacht club and boat docking area.

Part of the Central Park is also designated as a wetlands rehabilitation area to regenerate the natural environment.

Cultural Options

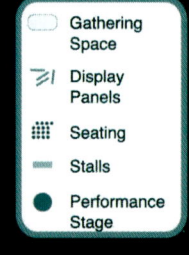

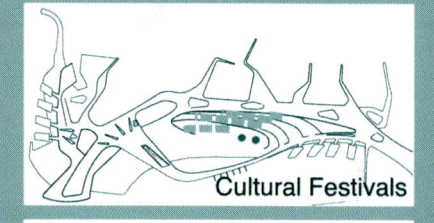

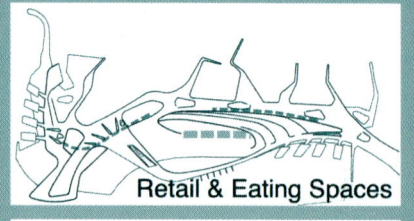

- Cultural Festivals
- Public Outdoor Exhibitions
- Retail & Eating Spaces
- Viewing Area for Fireworks

Legend:
- Gathering Space
- Display Panels
- Seating
- Stalls
- Performance Stage

Cultural Performances

Film Festival

Viewing areas onto Plaza

Arts Festivals

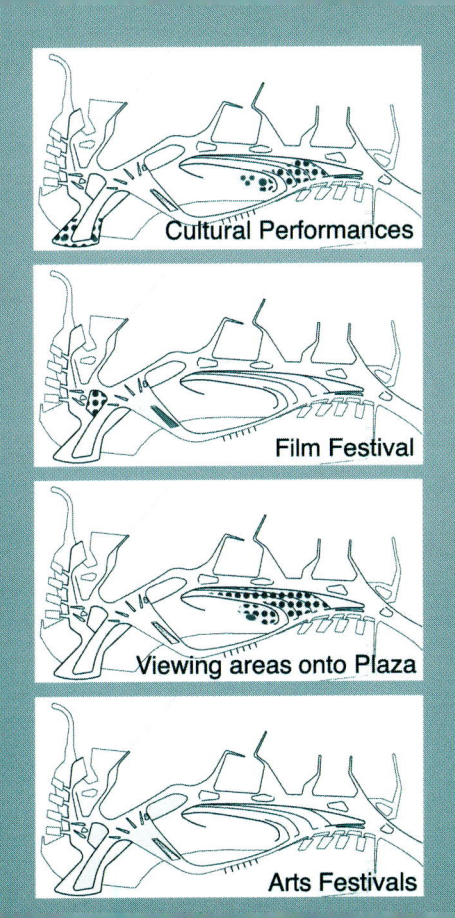

Cultural Events and Options

While there are special performance spaces in the design designated as cultural landmarks, such as the Opera House, the continuous extent of the "green jacket" allows a variety of cultural events and festivals to take place throughout the entire site. This flexibility allows the spaces around the site to be adapted according to the function or occasion, with provision for extensions if required.

	Winter	
Dec	Jan	Feb

Cultural Calendar

- 22 Dec - Winter Solstice
- 25 Dec - Christmas Day
- 1 Jan - New Year's Day
- 24 Jan - Chinese New Year

Events and Happenings in Hong Kong

Hong Kong Arts Festival

New Year Festivals

Usage of Centre Facilities

Opera House
Mediatheque
Museum of Arts
Arts Complex
Auditorium
Coliseum
Exhibition Hall
Cultural Plaza
Terraced Plazas

art festivals

Intensity of Activities in the Cultural Plaza

Winter Solstice Festival · Chinese New Year · Happy New Year

ecocells 42

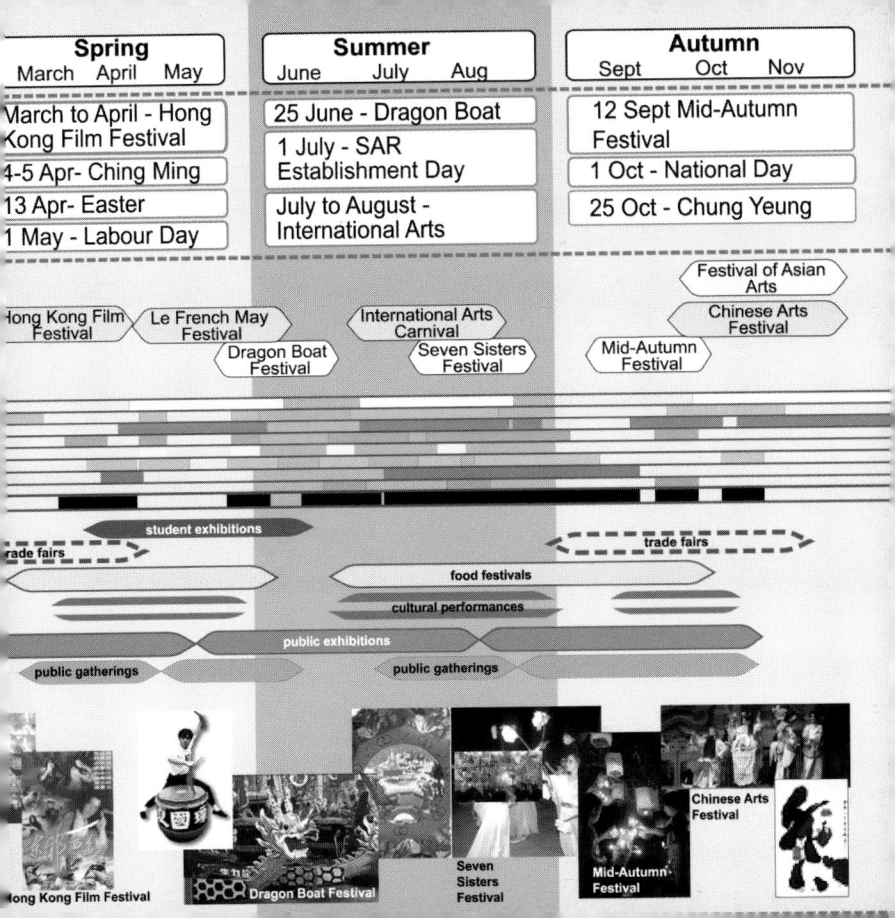

Spring	Summer	Autumn
March April May	June July Aug	Sept Oct Nov
March to April - Hong Kong Film Festival	25 June - Dragon Boat	12 Sept Mid-Autumn Festival
4-5 Apr - Ching Ming	1 July - SAR Establishment Day	1 Oct - National Day
13 Apr - Easter	July to August - International Arts	25 Oct - Chung Yeung
1 May - Labour Day		

- Hong Kong Film Festival
- Le French May Festival
- Dragon Boat Festival
- International Arts Carnival
- Seven Sisters Festival
- Mid-Autumn Festival
- Festival of Asian Arts
- Chinese Arts Festival

- student exhibitions
- trade fairs
- trade fairs
- food festivals
- cultural performances
- public exhibitions
- public gatherings
- public gatherings

Hong Kong Film Festival
Dragon Boat Festival
Seven Sisters Festival
Mid-Autumn Festival
Chinese Arts Festival

Landscape and Water Features

The design includes water features as integral parts of the landscape strategy to reinforce the strategic location of the site on the Kowloon waterfront. The new lagoon will integrate with the park, mangrove area and waterfront promenade to fulfil aesthetic and water management functions.

The variation of treatment of water bodies reinforces the different characters of the different zone within the site. The enclosed lagoon is a tranquil water body that invites reflection, while active water elements within the civic landscape around the Cultural Plaza, such as fountains, jets and sprays, provide a psychological cooling effect and encourage movement. Surface run-off from hard surfaces can be collected for use in the water features.

A demonstration "living machine" could be constructed in the park to showcase an ecologically sustainable treatment of waste water. Grey water from the developments could be treated on site using a combination of package treatment and final polishing through reed beds, finally discharging into the harbour through a series of native aquatic planting beds or used as an additional irrigation supply for the park. An adjacent visitors centre would serve to inform the public of the process and increase awareness of the fragility and importance of Victoria Harbour.

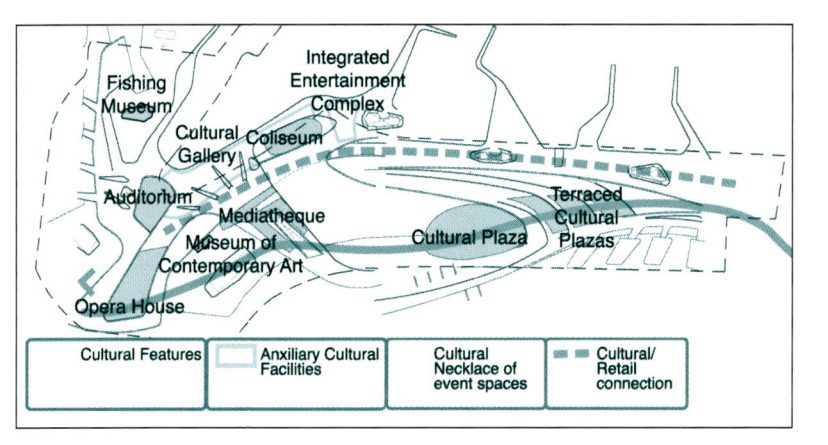

Cultural and Tourism Context

Given the existing cultural context in Kowloon, the emphasis of the proposal is on a more interactive form of culture. This is provided in the proposal in the form of performance spaces, cultural plazas and festival areas that will draw in and attract users from the surrounding locality as well as visitors and tourists.

The cultural features are integrated with not only the other districts of the development, but also incorporate elements of 'high' arts culture and 'low' street culture. It is by juxtaposing the spaces for these two different forms of culture that the scheme is able to successfully integrate a continuous cultural loop that will facilitate access and allow users to interface between the two.

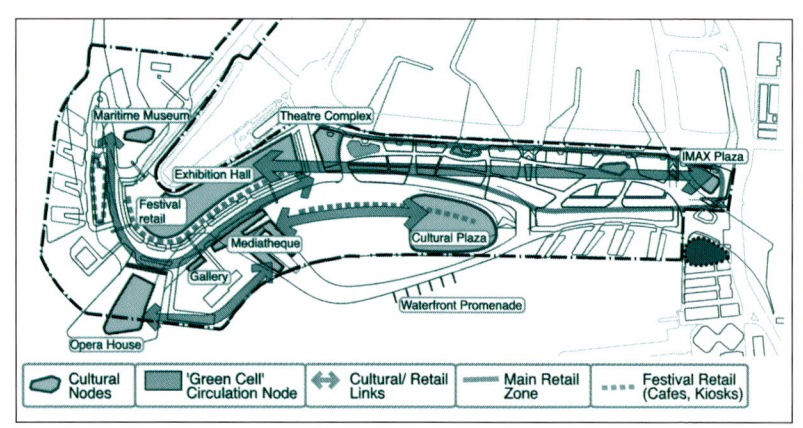

Top diagram legend:
- Cultural Nodes
- 'Green Cell' Circulation Node
- Cultural/Retail Links
- Main Retail Zone
- Festival Retail (Cafes, Kiosks)

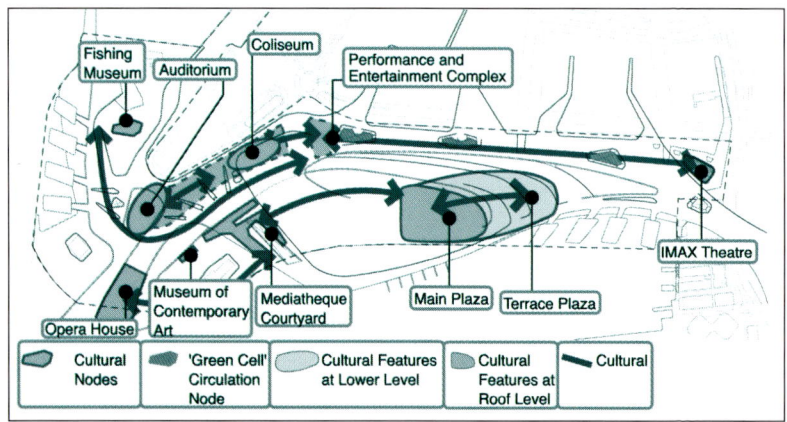

Top diagram labels: Maritime Museum, Theatre Complex, IMAX Plaza, Exhibition Hall, Festival retail, Mediatheque, Cultural Plaza, Gallery, Waterfront Promenade, Opera House

Bottom diagram legend:
- Cultural Nodes
- 'Green Cell' Circulation Node
- Cultural Features at Lower Level
- Cultural Features at Roof Level
- Cultural

Bottom diagram labels: Fishing Museum, Auditorium, Coliseum, Performance and Entertainment Complex, IMAX Theatre, Opera House, Museum of Contemporary Art, Mediatheque Courtyard, Main Plaza, Terrace Plaza

Cultural Features

The conceptual necklace forms the cultural link that consists of the following features:
- Opera House - a landmark quality performance space with views of Hong Kong and seating for over 2000 users.
- Mediatheque - an interactive multi-media gallery with digital exhibition spaces, resource library and auditorium.
- Museum of Contemporary Art - a cutting edge gallery to showcase the range of Hong Kong's culture.
- History of Fishing Museum - a showcase of a part of Hong Kong's history, complementing the Marina area.
- Coliseum - an outdoor viewing area set in the park for informal performances Indoor.
- Viewing Terrace - a gathering space at the foyer to the Coliseum and informal exhibition area.
- Amphitheatre - an open-air performance space with retractable canopy roof, set in the landscape with views to Hong Kong.
- Interactive Cultural Gallery - a special area for temporary exhibitions and trade fairs.
- Leisure and Entertainment Complex - an integrated complex with cinemas, leisure parks (skate parks, children's park) as interface between retail district and cultural features.
- IMAX theatre - located on Canton Road, this marks the street culture element of our proposal and will draw users into the retail area.
- Cultural Plaza - the main area for festive events and performances, public gathering, views of fireworks and recreation.
- Terraced Cultural Plazas - these provide additional gathering and viewing areas to the Cultural Plaza and Park, and provide a space for auxiliary cultural events.
- Event spaces in the park - informal gathering and performance spaces set in the landscape.

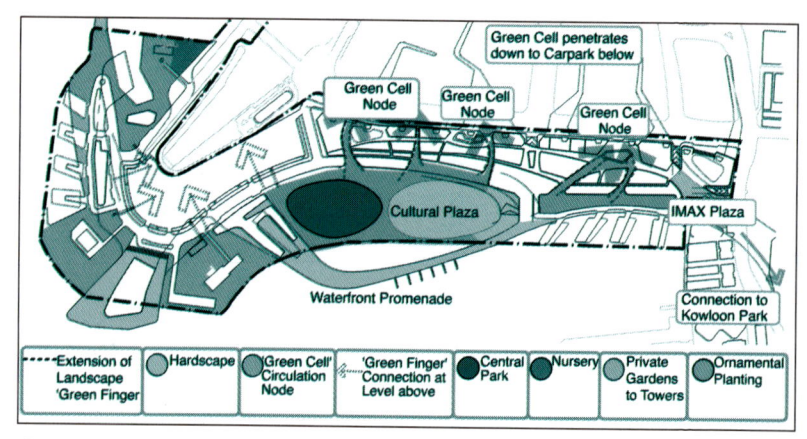

Landscape Concept

The landscape strategy aims to create a 21st century parkland setting for the cutting-edge cultural, residential and commercial developments of our proposal. The integration of the landscape will create a distinctive identity and sense of place within the various site components in West Kowloon, significantly reinforce the character of the site, enhance views to the harbour, help to modify the micro-climate and celebrate a culture of ecological sensitivity. By complimenting and providing a seamless link to the built form, the landscape proposal will facilitate movement and connectivity. In addition to offering a variety of amenity landscaped areas and key events areas, the landscape will also develop ecological links to enhance the surrounding context, including Kowloon Park, as the extension of a city-wide green network.

The features include:
• Extending ceremonial trees on either side along Austin Boulevard and streets leading off it, as extension of the green network at street level.

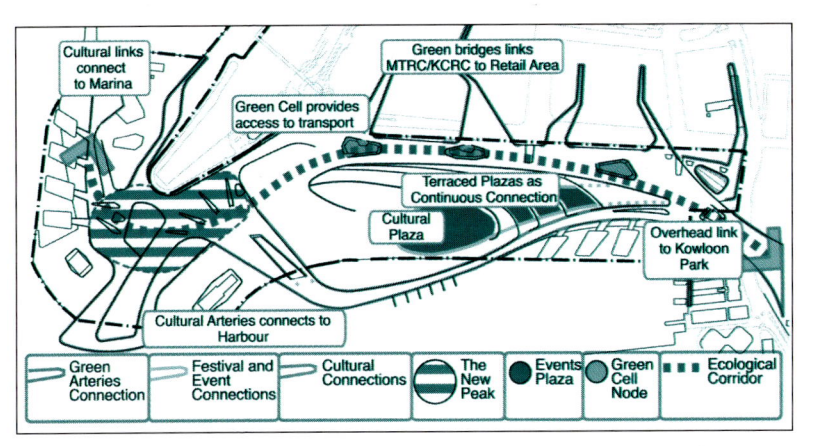

Diagram labels:
- Cultural links connect to Marina
- Green bridges links MTRC/KCRC to Retail Area
- Green Cell provides access to transport
- Terraced Plazas as Continuous Connection
- Cultural Plaza
- Overhead link to Kowloon Park
- Cultural Arteries connects to Harbour

Legend:
- Green Arteries Connection
- Festival and Event Connections
- Cultural Connections
- The New Peak
- Events Plaza
- Green Cell Node
- Ecological Corridor

- Using plazas as hard landscape to provide spaces for events, festivals, cafe/restaurant activities, retail and shaded rest areas.
- Providing localised community parks with play areas and sports facilities as gardens for local residents.
- Using artwork, water features and lighting as markers in the landscape to aid legibility and movement.
- Developing the waterfront promenade to create a continuous and pleasant link through the site and to the rest of the city.
- Pedestrian and bicycle pathways form a progression from the formal landscaped areas at the promenade and plazas to informal planted mounding areas and the ecological corridor.
- Celebrating the cultural and ecological diversity of Hong Kong through the creation of specific themed gardens such as tea gardens and pavilions, hillside habitats and mangrove planting areas.
- Integration of water bodies to provide a distinct character to different areas, such as the reflective lagoon or active water landscapes.
- Localised nursery area to service the park.

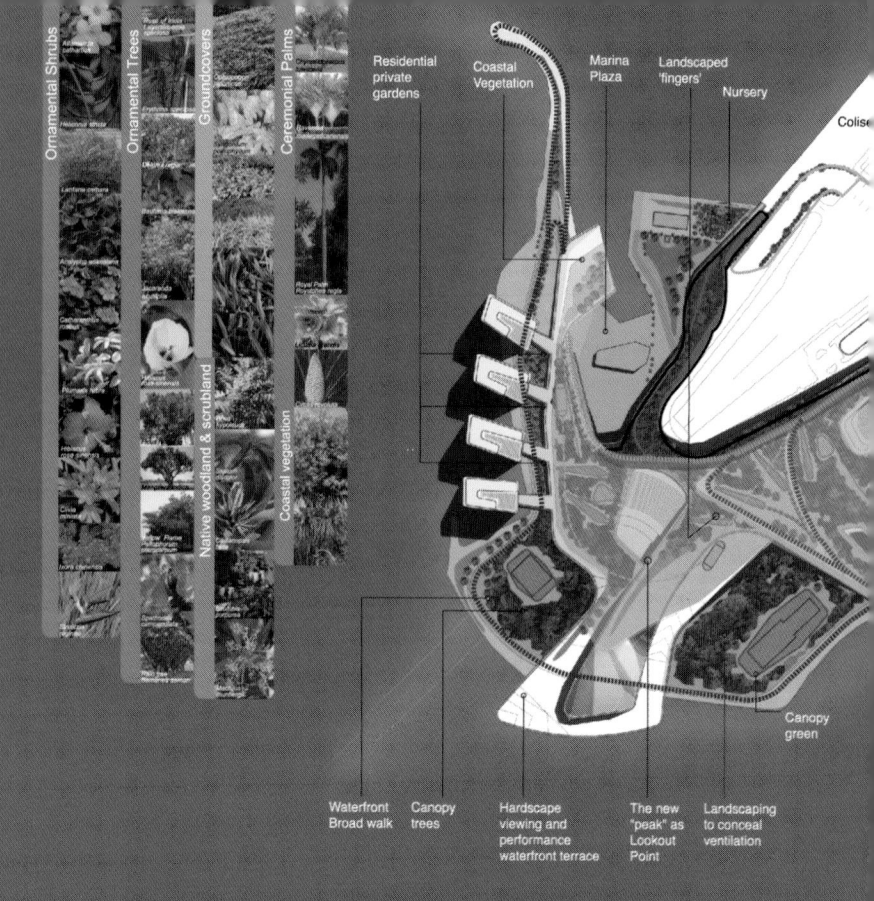

- Ornamental Shrubs
- Ornamental Trees
- Groundcovers
- Ceremonial Palms
- Native woodland & scrubland
- Coastal vegetation

- Residential private gardens
- Coastal Vegetation
- Marina Plaza
- Landscaped 'fingers'
- Nursery
- Coliseum
- Canopy green
- Waterfront Broad walk
- Canopy trees
- Hardscape viewing and performance waterfront terrace
- The new "peak" as Lookout Point
- Landscaping to conceal ventilation

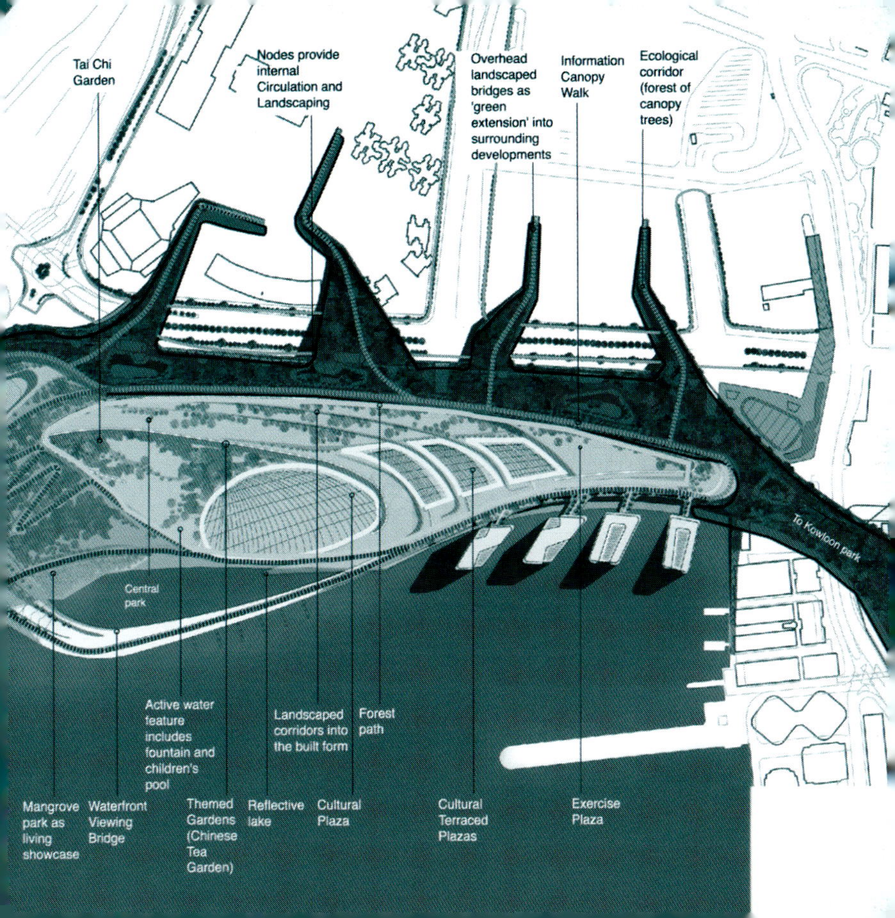

Tai Chi Garden
Nodes provide internal Circulation and Landscaping
Overhead landscaped bridges as 'green extension' into surrounding developments
Information Canopy Walk
Ecological corridor (forest of canopy trees)
Central park
To Kowloon park
Active water feature includes fountain and children's pool
Landscaped corridors into the built form
Forest path
Mangrove park as living showcase
Waterfront Viewing Bridge
Themed Gardens (Chinese Tea Garden)
Reflective lake
Cultural Plaza
Cultural Terraced Plazas
Exercise Plaza

Landscape and the built form

There are many psychological benefits to be gained from proximity to vegetation, notably the quality of spaces and views from buildings directly into tree canopies. By extending the landscape up to and into buildings, our proposal makes a strong visual and physical connection between the internal and external environment with a play on hard and soft materials from external plazas to covered walkways. Extending planting onto the development will also have ecological and amenity value in the form of landscaped balconies, landscaped links as 'green fingers' into the cultural and commercial areas, the "ecocell" nodes and internal landscape islands.

Natural landscape

The large extent of natural landscape in our development will illustrate the value and richness of natural habitats in Hong Kong and the importance of conserving them. Users can celebrate the diversity of Hong Kong through specific gardens that recreate microcosms of ecological systems, such as landscaped hills and a mangrove habitat area that links to the lagoon. The pedestrian pathways throughout the proposal can also be enhanced as nature walks with lookout points, canopy walkways, information points and visitors park centres.

Amenities in the landscape

Providing a diverse mix of park features will provide a dynamic intensive amenity landscape that will attract a constant flow of users. Large open spaces such as the open-air coliseum and civic hardscape areas such as the cultural plaza and terraced events plazas will cater for large events, including festivals and cultural celebrations. Smaller temporary events areas will act as auxiliary spaces with amenities such as cafes, restaurants and festive retail kiosks to activate the landscape. The cultural aspect of our proposal can be integrated with the landscape by developing a strong public art strategy that runs through the amenity landscape into the civic landscape.

Planting Strategy

The undulating levels of the proposal would be best enhanced with a variety of themed areas and landscape variations to provide interest and complement the built form. Planting types include:

Native woodland and scrubland
This planting type will form part of the ecological corridor and extend to Kowloon Park to wrap over, around and through the built form. Incorporating native trees and shrubs will help to recreate the Hong Kong woodland, ranging from coastal to hillside types. The plant material should be of local provenance from locally sourced seeds and cuttings to preserve the local gene pool.

Ornamental trees & palms
A range of ceremonial and canopy trees and palms will be used to provide structure, shade and seasonal interest within the parkland and to the surrounding context. Many of the species intended are commonly planted with parks and gardens across Hong Kong.

Ornamental shrubs and groundcover
A range of ornamental shrubs, groundcovers and climbers will provide texture and richness at different times of the year. These will provide diversity and be particularly suitable for themed areas.

Coastal vegetation
The extensive amount of coastal edge and the development of a lagoon area provides for the creation of areas of natural mangroves. Mangroves are a productive wetland habitat and featuring them as a demonstration area in the park could draw public attention to their precarious status in Hong Kong.

Feng-Shui woodland
This traditional woodland type will enhance the private gardens at the areas adjacent to the residential towers. Planting species that have some herbal and food values will also foster the spirit of community gardening.

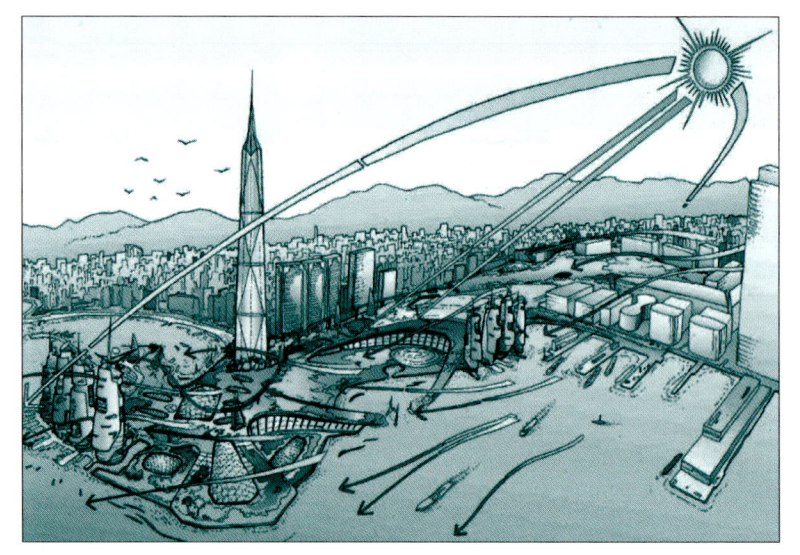

Ecological Design Strategy

Ecological design principles applied to the proposal are not just for their aesthetic value, but also have relevance in the fundamental planning and organic order. The proposal consists of a system of elevated park levels accessible by landscaped ramps, forming a "green jacket" that is a continuous horizontal urban landscape with links to surrounding parks and streets. This strategy is continued vertically in the sky gardens of the towers that rise above the linear park, assisting the establishment of a continuous eco-system.

Sustainable design features

The ecological features include:
- The landscaped links from Kowloon Park to the Ecological Corridor on site will encourage species migration and extend the urban landscape through physical continuity.
- Increasing the organic plant material component increases the site's biological diversity and hence its ecological stability.
- Lowering of the ambient air temperature through the evaporative processes of the plants acting as a cooling device.
- Plants act as windbreakers, especially on waterfront areas.
- The landscaping will absorb polluting emissions and carbon dioxide, converting it to oxygen through the process of photosynthesis and creating a healthier microenvironment around the development.
- Orientation of the residential towers on an east-west axis to reduce solar heat gain.
- Locating the service cores to the west side of the commercial towers to act as a massing shield to reduce solar heat gain.
- Plants can act as visual screens and sound diffusers, to break up pollution from the surrounding areas.
- Vertical planting on towers improves the microclimate at the facades of the building by providing additional shade and minimising heat reflection and glare into the building.
- "Ecocell" nodes will introduce natural daylight into all floors of the retail district and induce the flow of natural fresh ventilation.
- Planter boxes on at the side of the ramps in the "ecocell" nodes extend the landscaping into the building and connect with the landscape island at the base of the nodes to form a continuous internal green spiral.
- The landscaped roof utilises Hong Kong's year-round abundant rainfall to naturally irrigate the planting areas. Any shortfall in irrigation will be made up by reticulation systems.
- Circulation systems and built forms are arranged to minimise their impact on the functioning of the eco-system.

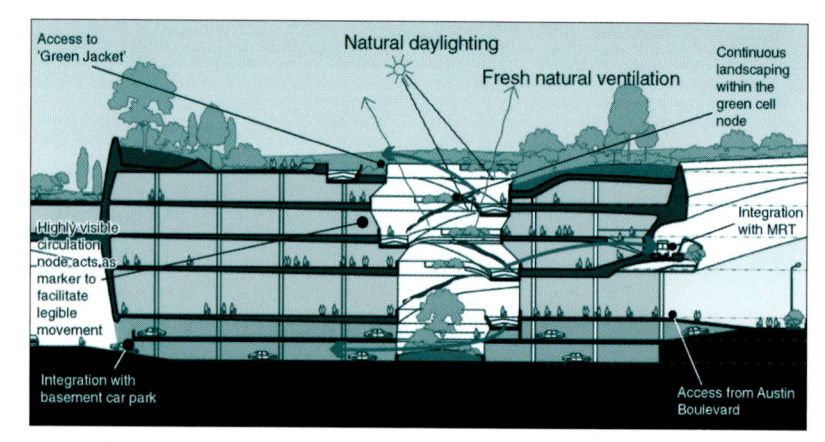

Diagram labels:
- Access to 'Green Jacket'
- Natural daylighting
- Fresh natural ventilation
- Continuous landscaping within the green cell node
- Highly visible circulation node acts as marker to facilitate legible movement
- Integration with MRT
- Integration with basement car park
- Access from Austin Boulevard

Retail Strategy

Introduction
- The retail and entertainment facilities are located to the north-east end of the site, with an extended street frontage along Austin Boulevard. Through integration of the retail areas with transportation infrastructure, leisure and entertainment facilities as well as cultural attractions, the development becomes a 24-hour district that allows for efficient use of space. Connections to the MTRC and KCRC developments and overhead passes to Tsim Tsa Tsui and Kowloon Park allow direct circulation to and through the development, making it a new regional hub.
- The retail district becomes a regional retail destination through careful integration with surrounding areas to enhance the locality. This is achieved through a seamless link of overhead landscaped bridges as part of the urban design concept to maximise the accessibility of the destination. Providing a range of quality retail spaces will ensure the development's adaptability to market needs.

Retail Proposal

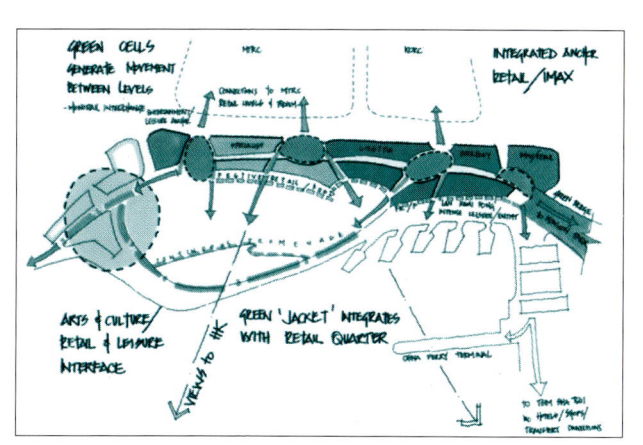

The retail proposal includes the following:

- 100,000 sqm retail, entertainment and leisure space.
- Subterranean car parking connected to the "ecocell" nodes.
- Subterranean servicing, providing distribution to all levels of specialist retail and entertainment zones.
- "Food Quarter" incorporating cafes / restaurants and bars with landscaped terraces, access to the park and panoramic views across to Hong Kong.
- Roof top park giving access to the retail zones via the "ecocell" nodes.
- Retail area linked by cultural and entertainment zones from theatre complex to IMAX theatre on Canton Road.
- Direct connection to the local transport infrastructure of Monorail stations located at each of the "ecocell" nodes.
- Pedestrian friendly environment with links through to the theatre, mediatheque, arts district and the waterfront.

Key to the successful integration of such distinct retail areas is achieved through identified streets that lead to the leisure, entertainment, commercial and cultural districts.

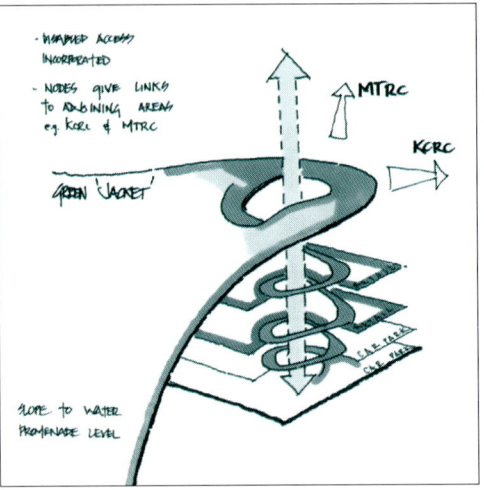

Retail Accessibility

The proposal achieves good accessibility by developing the integration of separate modes of transport to form a balanced, legible and sustainable network. Integrated transportation cores including proposed systems can be implemented in phases over a number of years.

"Ecocells"

Key to the success of efficent circulation through integrated transport networks are highly visible devices that act as markers in the landscape and bring together the various circulation systems. The "eco-cell" nodes can achieve this through their prominence in the landscape, drawing users to a single point that connects directly with the landscaped roof, retail and cultural districts, monorail station, central park, Austin Boulevard and parking at the basement level. The eco-cells may be distinguished through feature lighting and vegetation that extends from the landscaped roof down into the spaces of the building.

These "ecocells" are the vertical intergrators of the various layers in the building's design as a landscape sandwich. The "ecocells" are zones which bring in day-light to the lowest floor, provide sources of natural ventilations, collects rain-water which are filtered down through spiral ramps, integrating the biomass and vegetation using the ramps at all levels and are sites for the aerated eco-recycling ponds for the algae treatment of sewerage (see page 141).

Pedestrian circulation
An integral part of the concept is to provide a pedestrian dominant environment allowing "people movement" into, onto and through the development. All potential conflicts of movement between traffic, servicing and pedestrians are designed to a minimum. This is achieved through overhead landscaped bridges that extend to the surrounding. Circulation within the development is facilitated through overhead bridges, paths in the continuous landscaped roof and park and a waterfront link.

Commercial Development Strategy

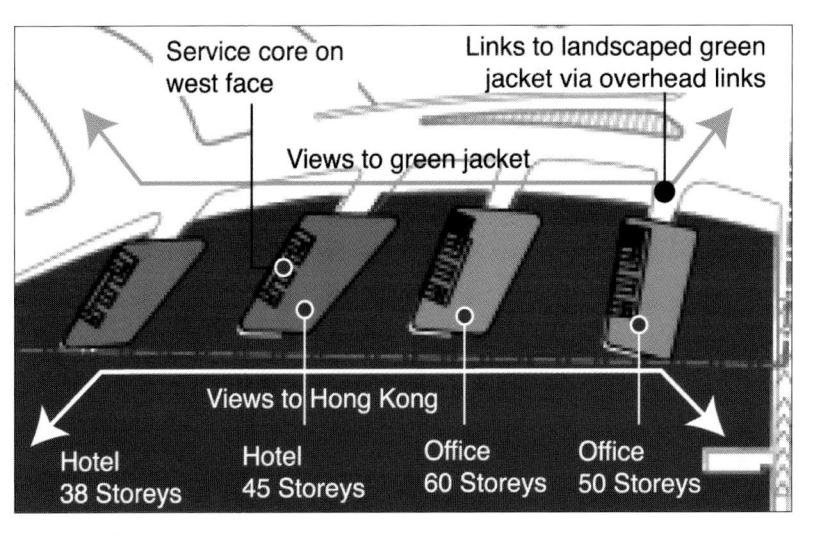

Service core on west face
Links to landscaped green jacket via overhead links
Views to green jacket
Views to Hong Kong
Hotel 38 Storeys
Hotel 45 Storeys
Office 60 Storeys
Office 50 Storeys

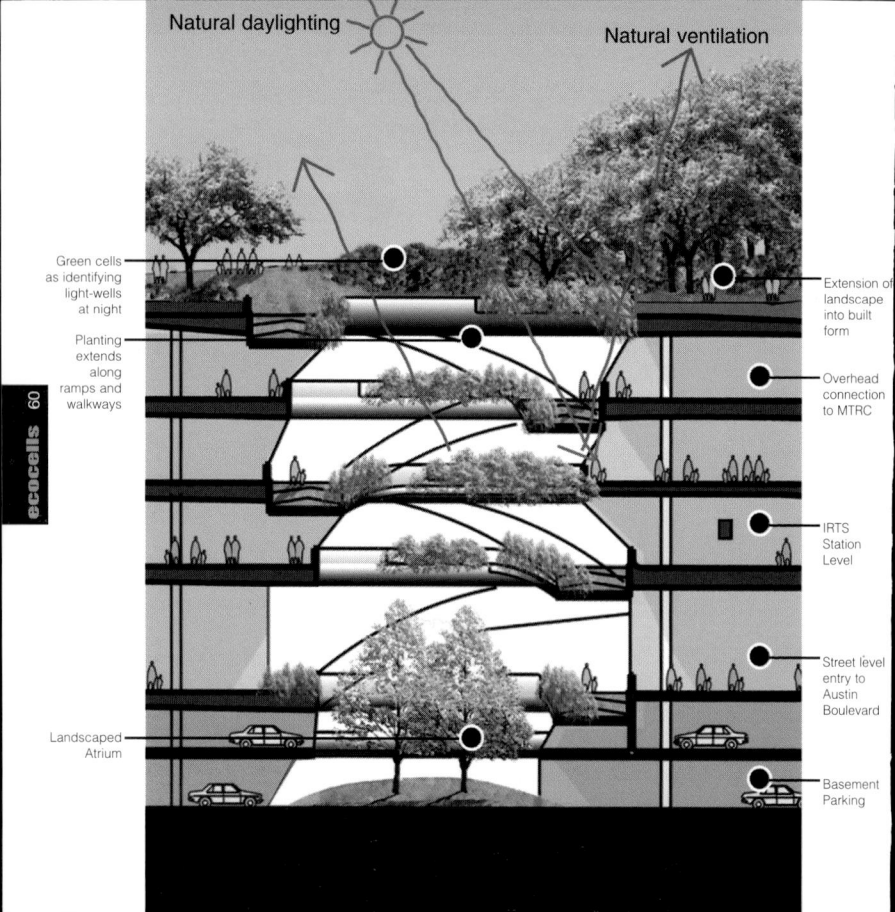

Natural daylighting • Natural ventilation

- Green cells as identifying light-wells at night
- Planting extends along ramps and walkways
- Landscaped Atrium

- Extension of landscape into built form
- Overhead connection to MTRC
- IRTS Station Level
- Street level entry to Austin Boulevard
- Basement Parking

ecocells 60

Office and Hotel Development Concept
The commercial development consists of office pier towers and hotel pier towers. These are connected at the "green jacket" landscaped roof level by overhead landscaped extensions that also form recreational areas.

Office and Hotel Development Features
The Pier Towers also contain a number of amenities
- Waterfront cafes, restaurant and ferry docking facilities at lower levels.
- Unique lobbies at the individual tower where the landscaped extensions from the roof level "green jacket" meet the development, providing green areas with views of Hong Kong harbour.
- Proximity to facilities and amenities such as Imax theatre, retail, Terraced Cultural Plazas and pedestrian connections to the surrounding area along Canton Road at Tsim Tsa Tsui.
- Accessibility to the pier tower is maximised with various modes of transport systems such as taxis, buses, the adjacent IRTS at the retail district and water ferries right up to the base of the piers.

The Towers
- The stepped built form of the Pier Tower maximises views.
- The orientation of the Pier Towers is angled to capture maximum views towards Hong. Kong Island, with service cores located on the west side to reduce effects of solar heat gain.
- The "Green Jacket" provides a continuous landscaped setting for the towers, and offers views of the greenery. The plantings at the service cores extends this landscaping vertically, forming a continuous green link.
- As extensions into the harbour within site boundaries, the Pier Towers directly address the Harbour and provide a dynamic built form interface.

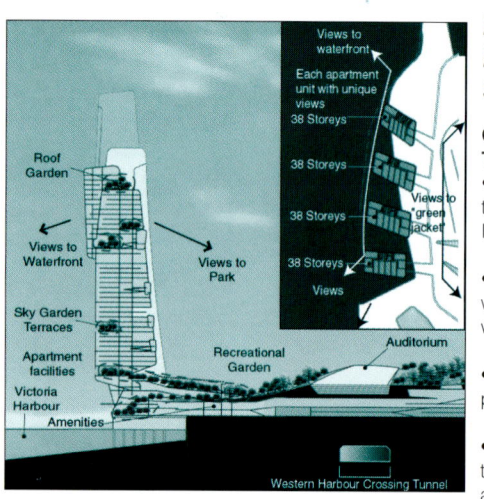

Residential Development Strategy

Concept for Residential Pier Towers
- Proximity to facilities and amenities such as the Marina, Integrated Community Centre.

- Ideal location on the waterfront with medium size developments within the vicinity.

- Open sky gardens and terraces provide vertical landscaping.

- The towers are oriented to capture views of Hong Kong Island and Victoria Harbour.

- Serviced with by public transportation systems, such as buses, taxis, water ferries and IRTS.

- Pedestrian connections through Waterfront Promenade (together with bicycle path) and "Green Jacket" at roof level.

Planning Strategy & Ecological-Design Orientation
- Built forms step down towards Hong Kong Island to maximise views and as a response to the scale of the Opera House.

- Pier towers are strategically located as a protective block from direct wind and sun to the activities at the "Peak".

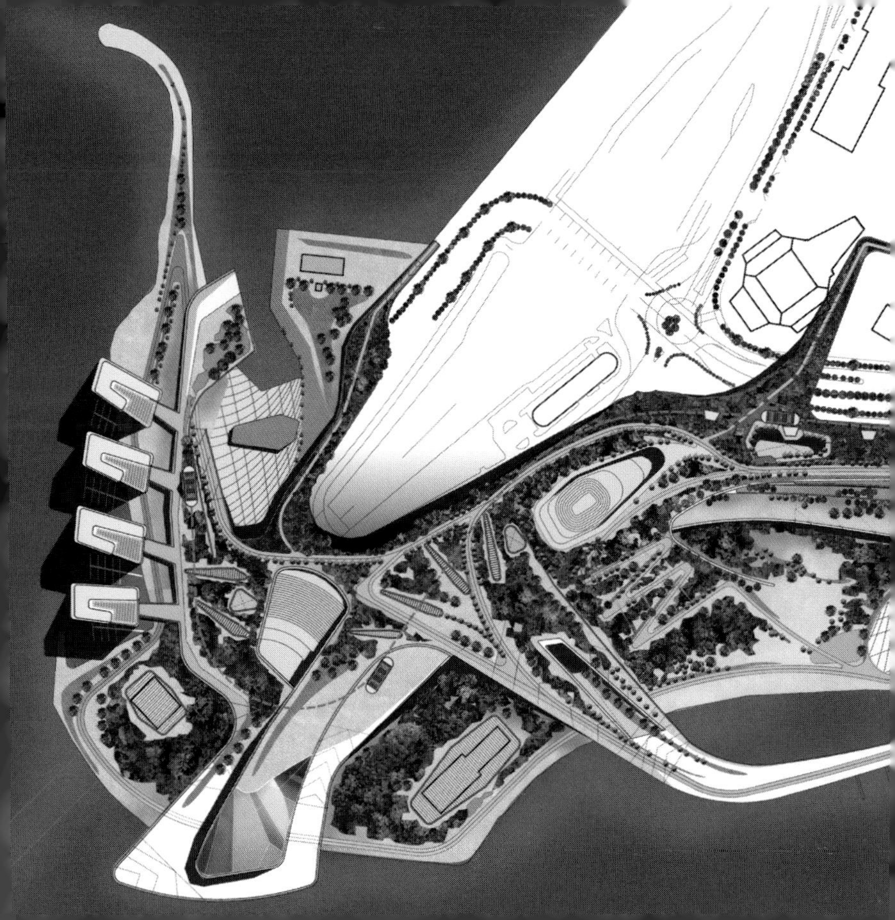

Community Strategy

Community Needs
Hong Kong is one of the most densely populated places on earth, with the Kowloon Peninsula the tightest squeeze of all as up to 2.12 million people try to fit into an area of 47 square metres. Bounded by physical limitations, many of the city's mass public housing schemes are forced upwards with an increasing emphasis on vertical economies of scale. Given the constraints on individual space when many family units exist with up to 3 generations in an apartment, private space is at a premium. Conversely, it is only in the open communal spaces that most residents can find a measure of privacy, which is why many parts of the city remain open 24 hours a day to feed this need for a public retreat.

Community Features
The following are the community features:
- The "Green Jacket" offers many public spaces and will become a local icon, attracting a broad range of users to the many facilities of our development.
- Integration of the development with surrounding areas, allows easy access and circulation.
- Provision of landmark public spaces for gathering and meeting.
- Event spaces at the cultural plazas for festivals and celebrations.
- Large expanse of landscaped recreational space such as the central park, pedestrian and cycle pathways, marina, active water features, children's play areas and theme gardens.
- An "Ecological Corridor" provides a valuable informative experience and can be utilised for school excursions.
- Wide range of facilities and amenities in the retail district will service users needs.
- Links with the cultural facilities will foster appreciation of culture and encourage community participation.

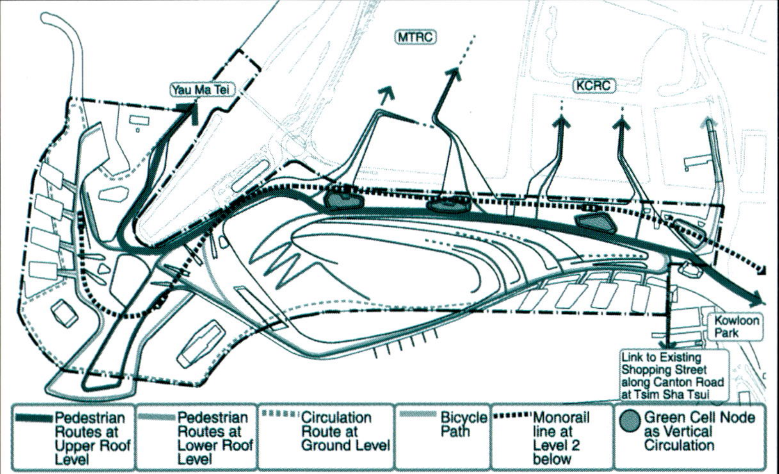

ecocells

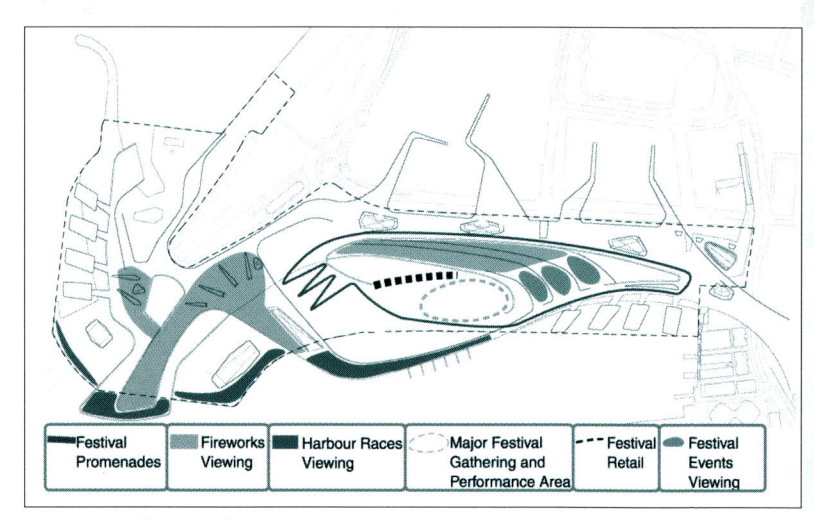

Legend:
- Festival Promenades
- Fireworks Viewing
- Harbour Races Viewing
- Major Festival Gathering and Performance Area
- Festival Retail
- Festival Events Viewing

Recreational Strategy

This vast and undulating landscape provided by the "green jacket" allows provisions for large open spaces for recreation and a variety of specific spaces to capture the needs of different user groups. The recreational areas will include:
- Roof Jacket (cycle and pedestrian paths, excercise plaza, Marina with fishing jetty, outdoor cafes, restaurant, kiosk and ferry cruises, informative forested walks through the Ecological Corridor, incorporation of linked retail activities, such as children's play area, skate park, putting green.
- Landscaped Parks (pebble stone parks for reflexology exercise, quiet park provides Tai Chi in a calm setting, water related activities at the water park, landscaped trails, Central Park as a place for contemplation.

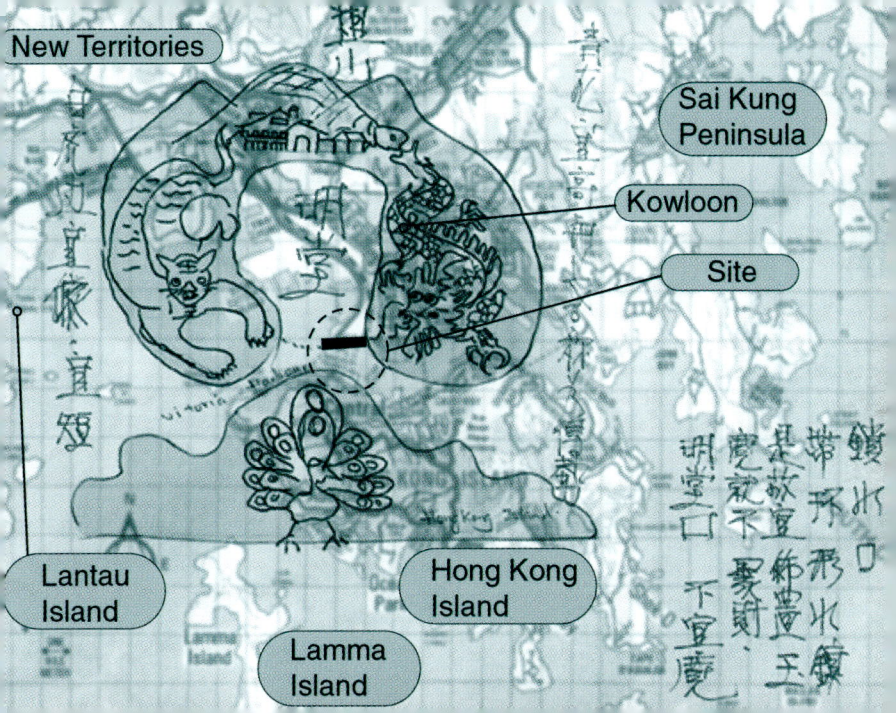

- New Territories
- Sai Kung Peninsula
- Kowloon
- Site
- Lantau Island
- Hong Kong Island
- Lamma Island

Feng Shui Strategy

Feng Shui Site Analysis

Feng Shui is a philosophy of Chinese origin, which maintains that the configuration of the earth shape the affairs of the people that live among them. Chinese geomancy is the art of finding and providing such a situation, or living in tune with the natural setting and the energy of the earth, rather than fighting the laws of nature. Feng Shui helps man utilize the earth's natural forces and balance 'yin' and 'yang' to achieve good 'qi', which renders health and vitality. Very often good feng shui is achieved through the combination of common sense and good taste in the conception of space, placement of correct site and best use of structure. Excellent living conditions contribute to good health, which often leads to success and prosperity.

The classical method for detecting the best Feng Shui locations commences with the search for Dragons which are symbolic of 'mountains' and therefore epitomised by elevated landforms. The true Dragon of the East will also be complemented by another geographical feature, to the west of the site and known as the Tiger. The Dragon will be the higher point, merging into the lower, gentler slopes of the Tiger. More usually, however, the Dragon and Tiger are perceived as two distinguishable hills. Ideally, these will form a pair of hills meeting in a horse-shoe or bow shaped formation. In an ideal site, wherever there is a high-rise building or mountain range behind an aforesaid site, it is considered as the Black Tortoise of the North which can be conceived of as a supporter. The Black Tortoise at the back, i.e. the North, supports the locations, and the vermilion Phoenix in the South is a small 'footstool' type formation. When all four directions of the compass and animals are present, the symbolism is complete.

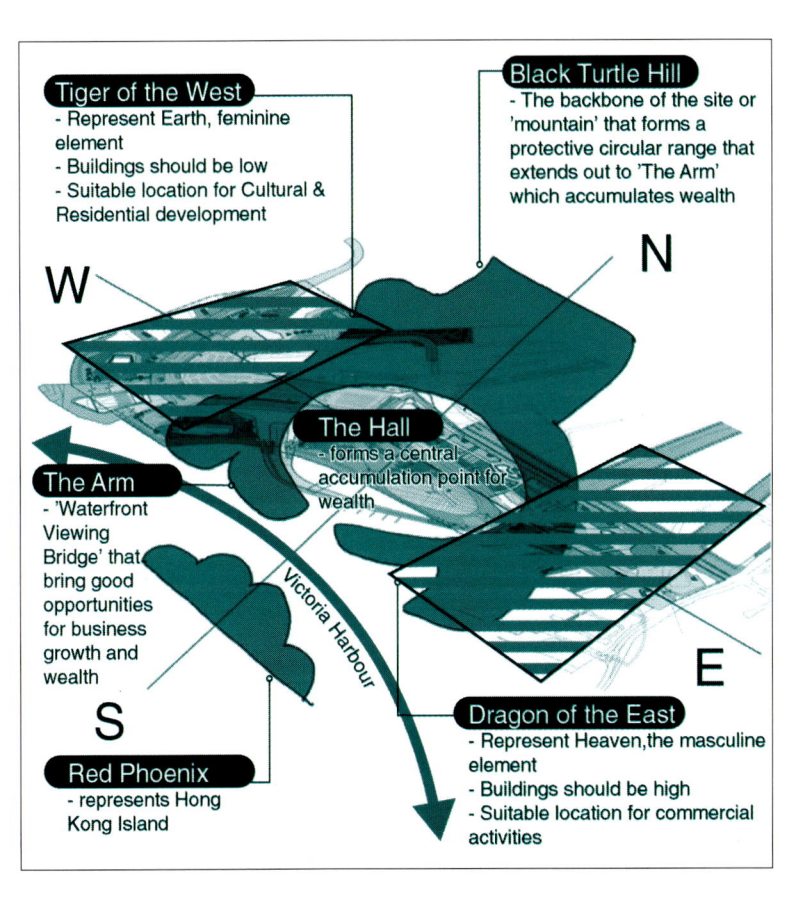

Tiger of the West
- Represent Earth, feminine element
- Buildings should be low
- Suitable location for Cultural & Residential development

Black Turtle Hill
- The backbone of the site or 'mountain' that forms a protective circular range that extends out to 'The Arm' which accumulates wealth

W

N

The Hall
- forms a central accumulation point for wealth

The Arm
- 'Waterfront Viewing Bridge' that bring good opportunities for business growth and wealth

Victoria Harbour

S

E

Red Phoenix
- represents Hong Kong Island

Dragon of the East
- Represent Heaven, the masculine element
- Buildings should be high
- Suitable location for commercial activities

This particularly applies to the proposal where the mountain "zhi yin shan" and the highrise development behind at the north can be considered as a supporting Black Turtle and Hong Kong Island to the south symbolises a red phoenix. The reclaimed land area at the eastern side near Tsim Sha Tsui is termed the Green Dragon of the East. Thus the West side of the site is near 'Mong Kok' and is termed the White Tiger. Therefore, the Dragon of East is where all the high rise complexes and hotels are located. On the other hand, the lower ground of the Tiger of the West is where all the Apartments, Opera House, Marina with outdoor cafes, restaurant and Maritime Museum are located. Here, the Dragon and Tiger are in embrace, which is said to be the most fortuitous aspect of all.

The harmonious flow of water creates wonderful and auspicious feng shui energies that bring opportunities for business growth, when oriented correctly, water and all the various manifestations of water that are within views of the main door or entrance of a building attracts good fortune to the said site. This is because the flow of water is believed to mirror the flow of the invisible 'chi' currents that swirl around the earth. Therefore, from the proposed site, the proposed scheme areas seem to be embraced by water of the Victoria Harbour which is good feng shui.

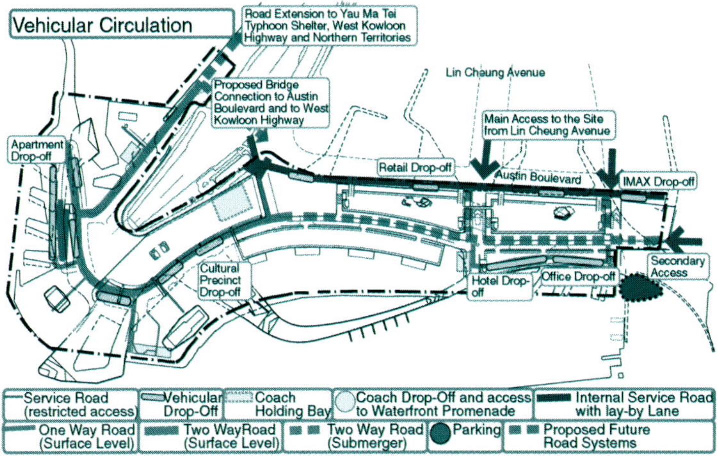

Vehicular Circulation

- Road Extension to Yau Ma Tei Typhoon Shelter, West Kowloon Highway and Northern Territories
- Proposed Bridge Connection to Austin Boulevard and to West Kowloon Highway
- Lin Cheung Avenue
- Apartment Drop-off
- Retail Drop-off
- Main Access to the Site from Lin Cheung Avenue
- Austin Boulevard
- IMAX Drop-off
- Cultural Precinct Drop-off
- Coach Holding Bay
- Hotel Drop-off
- Office Drop-off
- Secondary Access

Legend:
- Service Road (restricted access)
- Vehicular Drop-Off
- Coach Holding Bay
- Coach Drop-Off and access to Waterfront Promenade
- Internal Service Road with lay-by Lane
- One Way Road (Surface Level)
- Two Way Road (Surface Level)
- Two Way Road (Submerger)
- Parking
- Proposed Future Road Systems

ecocells 71

Vehicular Access and Circulation Strategy

A lay-by lane is proposed along Austin Boulevard to create an intermediate lane for drop-off areas, delivery bays and waiting zones. This would reduce congestion on Austin Boulevard, and create spatial opportunities for landscaping to enhance the character of the street. The main access to the development would be via Lin Cheung Road, since traffic from the site can access Hong Kong Island through the Western Harbour Crossing and Western Kowloon and N.T. via West Kowloon Highway, and vice versa. Lin Cheung Road also connects with Jordan Road which links with primary distributor roads such as Nathan Road, Gascoigne Road, Chatham Road, Cross Harbour Tunnel, etc. to other parts of the SAR territories.

There is the option of access from the junction at Austin Road / Canton Road but it should be noted that currently both Austin Road and Canton Road are already operating at capacity especially during peak hours. Moreover, the scope for increasing the capacity of the junction is constrained by nearby existing private development. As a result, the junction would only be providing auxiliary services for traffic to / from the southern parts of Kowloon and Hong Kong Island. Another possible access is via the roundabout junction adjacent to the Western Harbour Crossing Toll Plaza. This would provide an alternative access directly to the western part of the development area near the Yau Ma Tei Typhoon Shelter.

Internal circulation roads are located at Level 1 and there is a ramp down to Basement 1 beneath the mounded central park. Clearance for these submerged roads is more than adequate at 4.0 metres. Private roads allow secure controlled access to the pier towers, both residential and commercial. There is also a provision for a future road connection to Yau Ma Tei Typhoon Shelter, with a proposed overhead bridge to link back to the roundabout at Austin Boulevard.

Legend: Car parking (retail) | Car Parking (office/hotel) | Car Parking (recreational/park) | Car Parking (cultural zone) | Coach parking and drop off | ↔ Parking ingress and egress

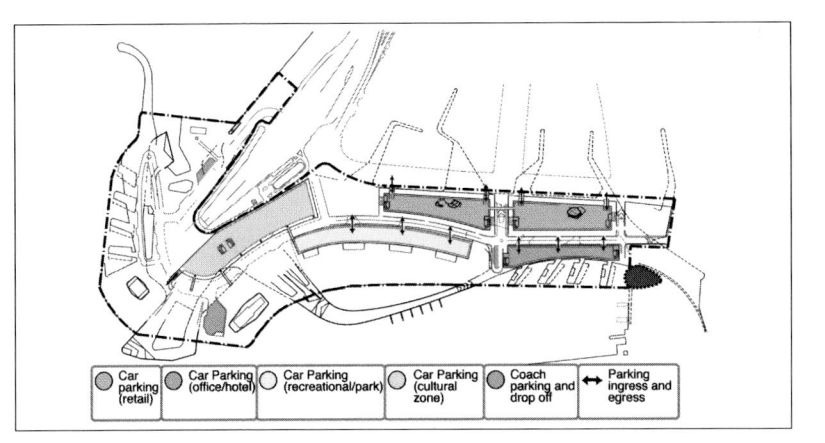

Parking and Loading Facilities

The scheme comprises a mixed-use series of developments to provide a vehicle-free environment with parking and loading facilities provided underground as far as practicable.

Passenger pick-up/drop-off laybys will be provided near the major activity areas such as the retail district, Opera House, piers towers, etc. Servicing facilities will be provided at Level 1 or Basement 1 Level mainly to serve routine goods delivery to individual development buildings.

The designated coach parking areas will also be used as holding areas during large functions and major events within the area.

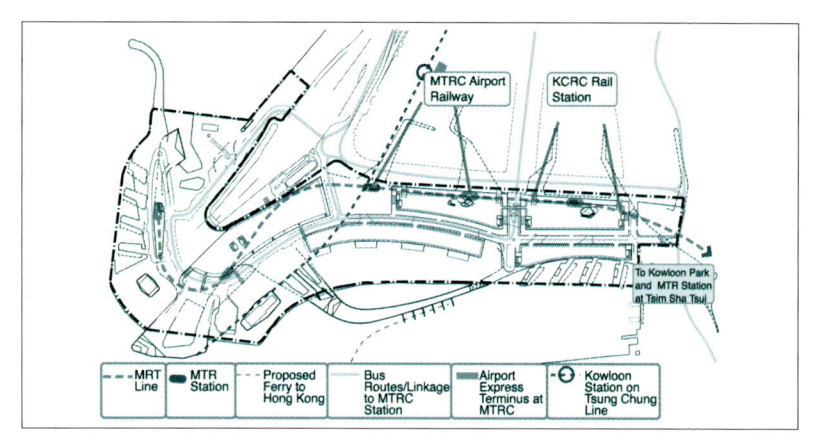

Legend:
- — — MRT Line
- ■ MTR Station
- - - - Proposed Ferry to Hong Kong
- Bus Routes/Linkage to MTRC Station
- ▇ Airport Express Terminus at MTRC
- ⊙ Kowloon Station on Tsung Chung Line

Public Transport Facilities
In order to provide a better environment and enhance the efficient use of road space, visitors are encouraged to use public transport to access the area. Different modes of public transport are already available:

Heavy Rail
The MTR Airport Railway Kowloon Station and the future KCR West Kowloon Station will also be located opposite the development area, carrying people from various parts of the territories to West Kowloon. Direct pedestrian linkages will be provided to connect the development area with the railway stations.

Other Public Transport Services
Public transport interchanges will be provided at both the MTR and KCR rail stations, providing interchange facilities for different types of public transport including franchised bus service, minibus and taxi services, etc. In addition, pick up / drop off areas will be provided at appropriate locations within the development area to provide easy access to our proposed facilities.

IRTS
The proposed Internal Rapid Transit System will serve both the new and 'old' arts and cultural district providing an efficient system connecting Tsim Sha Tsui. At the Austin Boulevard / West Kowloon Highway junction a 'leg' of track will potentially serve the identified Secondary Developments site (existing Typhoon Shelter). The elevated IRTS will not conflict with the existing traffic routes.

The proposaled IRTS would offer numerous benefits:
- Strategic links to key destinations within the district.
- The proposed system will be open to all providing convenient and safe mobility.
- Environmentally friendly, zero emission fleets electrically powered.
- Trains glide quietly giving unobtrusive sound transmission.
- Elevated tracks, accidents between surface traffic and pedestrians are impossible.
- Spatial requirements along routes are small allowing sufficient space to upgrade roads with landscaping.
- The proposed urban rapid transit system would be fully automated using state of the art technology.

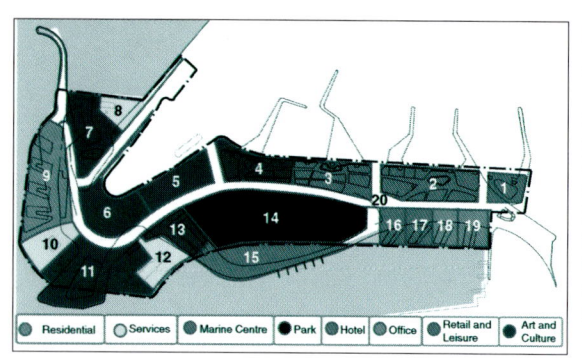

Parcellation and Areas

Based on the masterplan concept, the extensive reclaimed site area is subdivided into parcels of land that correspond to the type of land use as designated in the masterplan.

The purpose of the parcellation is to ensure that:

- By providing a web of roads around the land parcels, the land parcels can be effectively serviced and proper means of escape and fire fighting strategy can be maintained.

- Parcellation is an effective means for the Government to control development density on the site. The parcellation provides a broad guideline on which a framework of options to redevelop the areas by private / public participation can be established and the sequence of phasing of development can be easily controlled.

- The land parcels enable the government to allocate land by auction or by other means.

Nineteen lots of land parcels have been developed and their development density and respective land uses are indicated on the above diagram. Land parcels 1 to 6, 11, and 13 to 15 are zoned as shopping and cultural land use, taking up 18.8 ha. of the site with a development density of around plot ratio 1:3.2 on average. Land parcels 16 to 19 with 4.1 ha. are zoned as office and hotel areas with a much higher plot ratio of 8. Meanwhile, the residential areas and marine centre on parcels 7 and 9 would be developed up to a plot ratio 6.5.

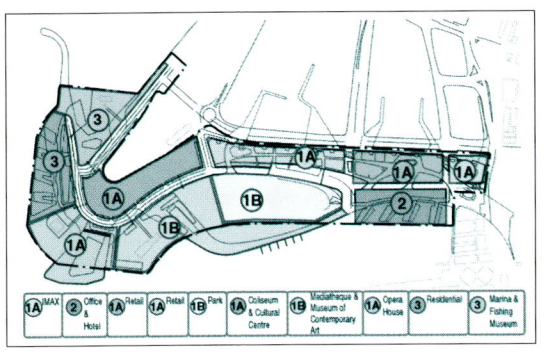

Phasing

The Outline Phasing Plan presents a progressive implementation for a workable package of land uses, including an enhanced waterfront, new quality civic and commercial developments, extensive open space provision and reserves for essential circulation and access.

The development phasing has been designated as follows:

• The stretch of land at the waterfront, which forms the basic shape of the masterplan, will be developed as the first phase of the project. This zone would entail commercial spaces, open spaces, and cultural functions with the Opera House as the landmark for the site. This phase is the longest and most difficult phase as the main infrastructure within the site would need to be implemented to facilitate the phases that follow. The retail development is included in the first phase to self-finance the cultural and open spaces.

• With the shops and entertainment facilities in place, the complexes of hotel and offices would be developed as the next phase. These will in turn support the shops and draw a large volume of users into the proposal.

• It is expected that the waterfront promenade at the south side which includes a viewing bridge will be completed when the hotel and offices are ready for occupation.

• The residential development with an adjacent marina will be developed as the last phase. With other facilities in place, the residential area will attract substantial premiums to justify the value of this precious piece of land.

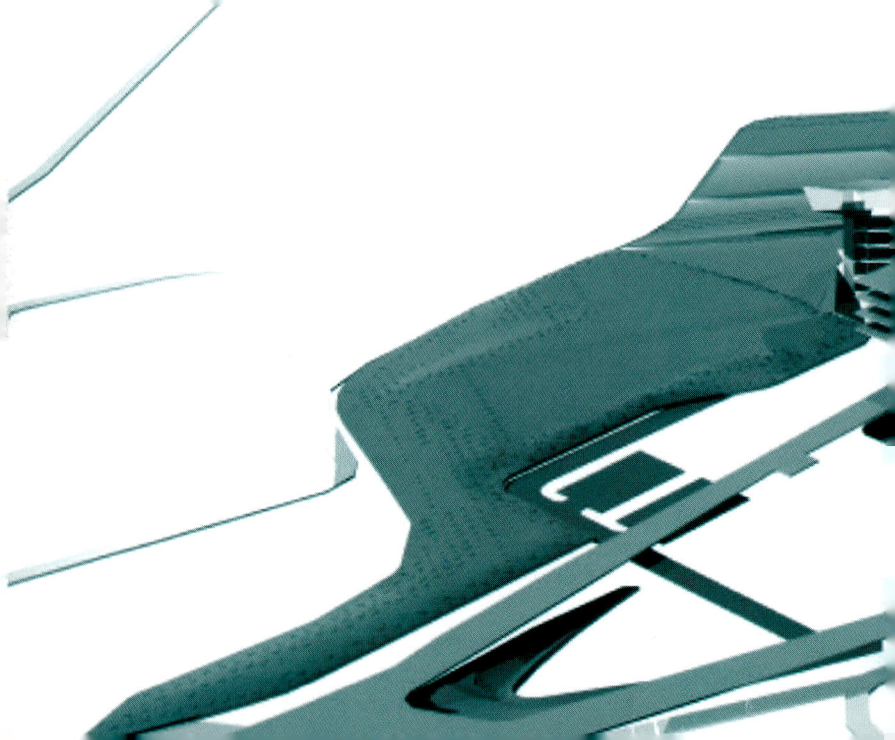

3. FNWI Development, University of Amsterdam Urban Ecosystem

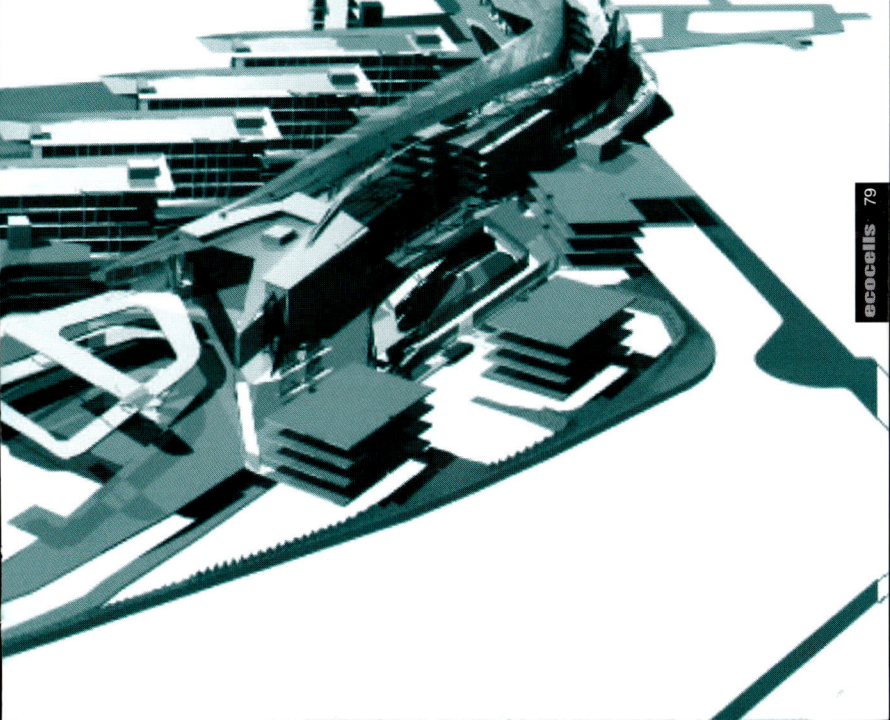

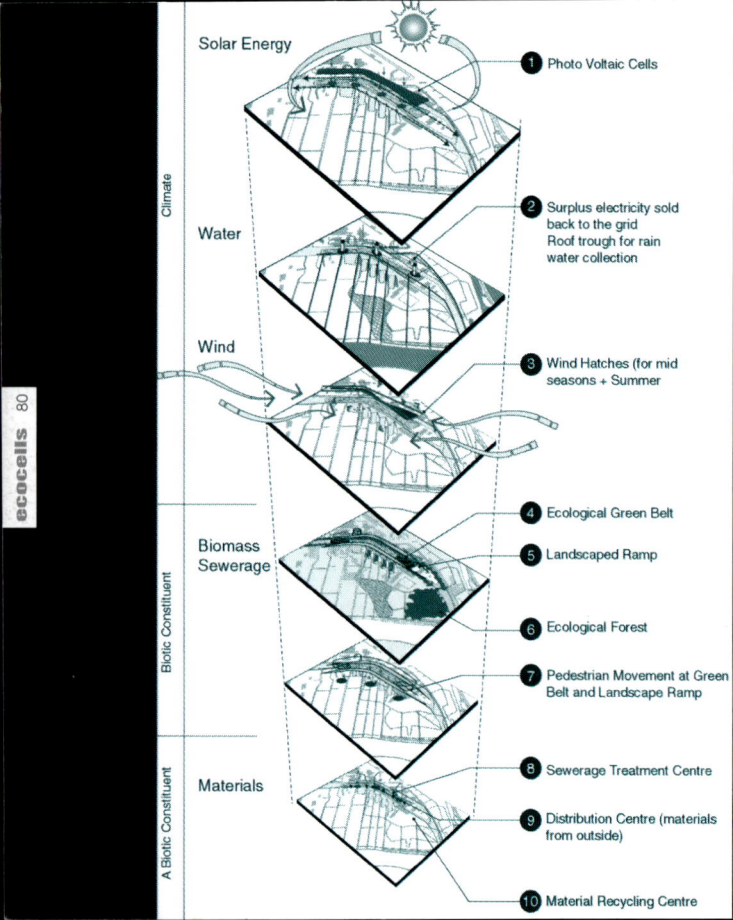

ecocells

Climate

Solar Energy
1. Photo Voltaic Cells

Water
2. Surplus electricity sold back to the grid. Roof trough for rain water collection

Wind
3. Wind Hatches (for mid seasons + Summer)

Biotic Constituent

Biomass Sewerage
4. Ecological Green Belt
5. Landscaped Ramp
6. Ecological Forest
7. Pedestrian Movement at Green Belt and Landscape Ramp

A Biotic Constituent

Materials
8. Sewerage Treatment Centre
9. Distribution Centre (materials from outside)
10. Material Recycling Centre

The Urban Ecosystem

The design's key feature is a unique "interactive zone" at Level 2. At this zone all the users of the facility are encouraged to meet and interact here. This "cultural" zone is designed to be a pleasurable space for education, entertainment, eating, etc.

Our design here is designed as an "urban ecosystem", to create an environmentally responsive holistic design solution for the WTCW site that considers the facility in terms of flow of people, water, vegetation, energy, and waste.

All architecture should relate ecologically to the natural environment as a whole. Simply stated, we must seek in our design a directed contribution towards a sustainable ecological future.

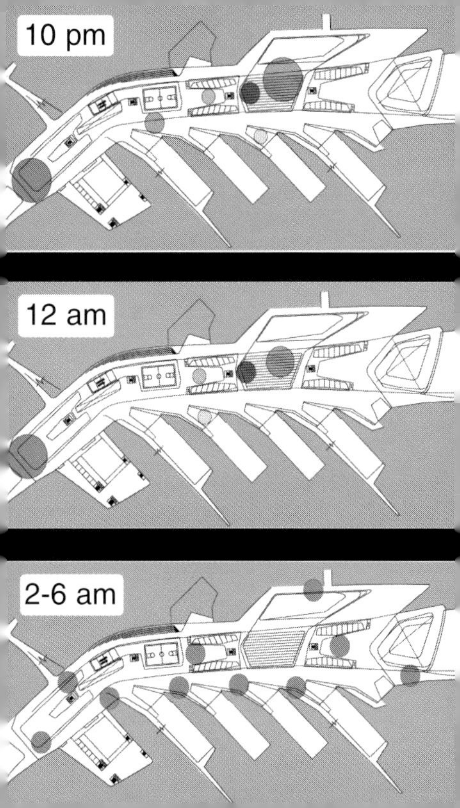

10 pm

12 am

2-6 am

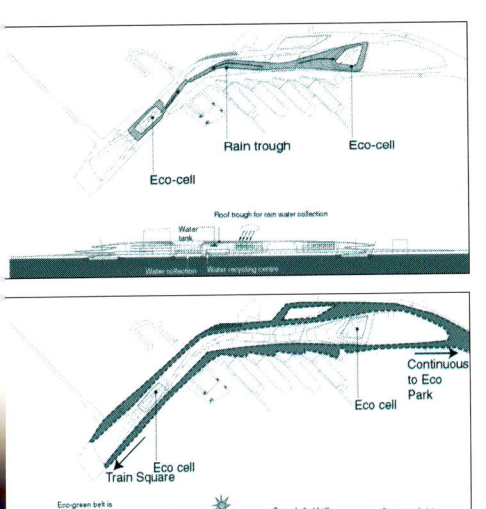

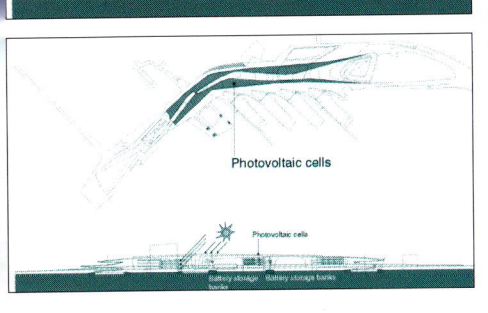

In the ecological approach these flows are considered:

Flow of Water
Water is collected in a trough on the concourse roof and drained into the "ecocells" where they are treated for reuse. The roofs to the department blocks are landscaped to reduce the rate of water run-off into the ground.

Flow of vegetation
Continuous vegetation (from the ecological park on the east to the station plaza) is connected via the green corridor on level 3.

Flow of energy
Embedded in the glass of the roof are photovoltaic cells which provide renewable energy source. Excess energy is stored in battery centres within the site, which may be sold back to the grid. The stored energy may be used for charging of electric buggies that transport users and circulate the concourse.

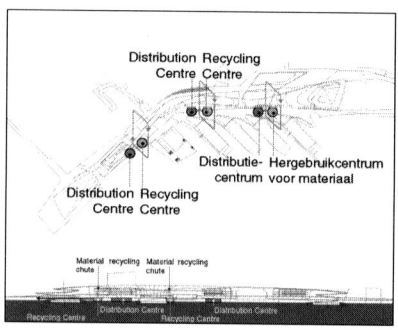

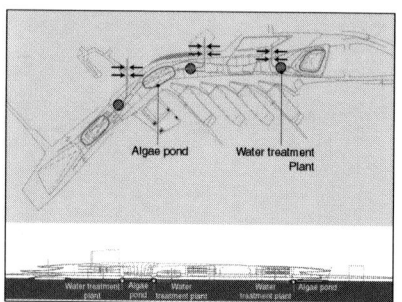

Flow of material
Recycling centres are provided on Level 1. These are equipped with chutes from the upper floors with in-built waste separators for different recycling materials.

Flow of sewage
Sewage effluence is channelled into the algae ponds within the "ecocells" and treated to produce fresh water.

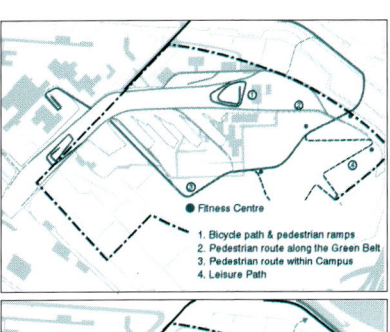

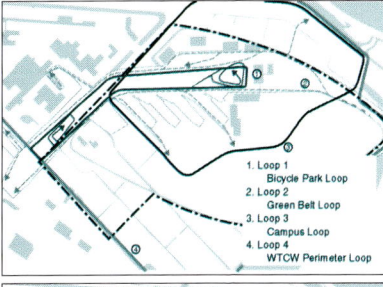

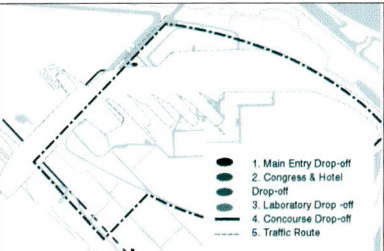

Flow of people (circulation)

Pedestrian:
The concourse on Level 2 serves as the main pedestrian movement level and cultural zone.

Cyclists:
The green belt would be accessible to cyclists via ramps from Level 1 and 2, providing an uninterrupted cycling path to and fro from the station and between buildings along the interaction spine. Instead of cycling, users can use foot scooters.

Vehicular:
Motorised vehicles are confined within Level 1. Various pick-up and drop-off locations are available close to the vertical circulation points.

- Fitness Centre
1. Bicycle path & pedestrian ramps
2. Pedestrian route along the Green Belt
3. Pedestrian route within Campus
4. Leisure Path

1. Loop 1 — Bicycle Park Loop
2. Loop 2 — Green Belt Loop
3. Loop 3 — Campus Loop
4. Loop 4 — WTCW Perimeter Loop

1. Main Entry Drop-off
2. Congress & Hotel Drop-off
3. Laboratory Drop-off
4. Concourse Drop-off
5. Traffic Route

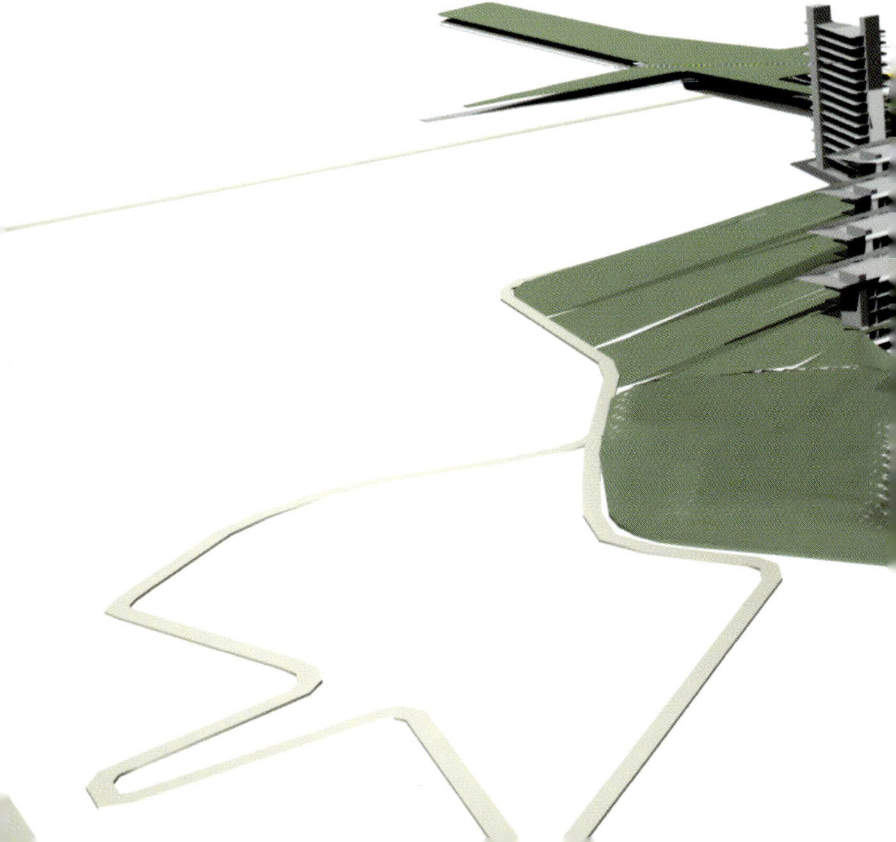

View of builtform from North-East

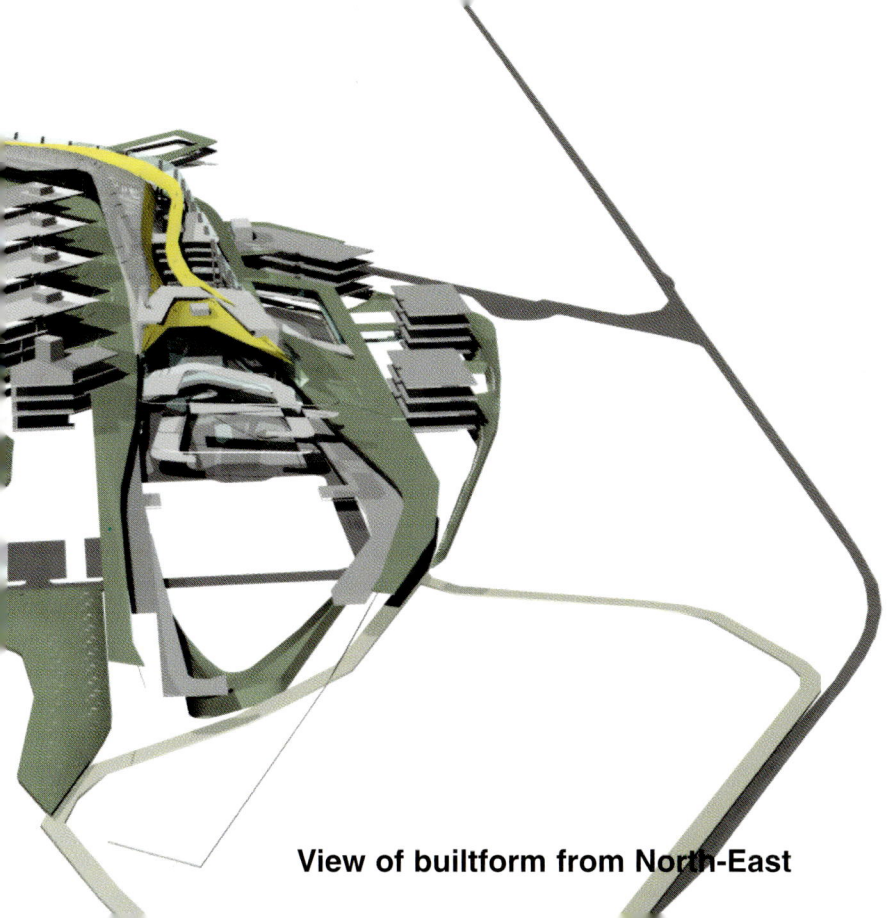

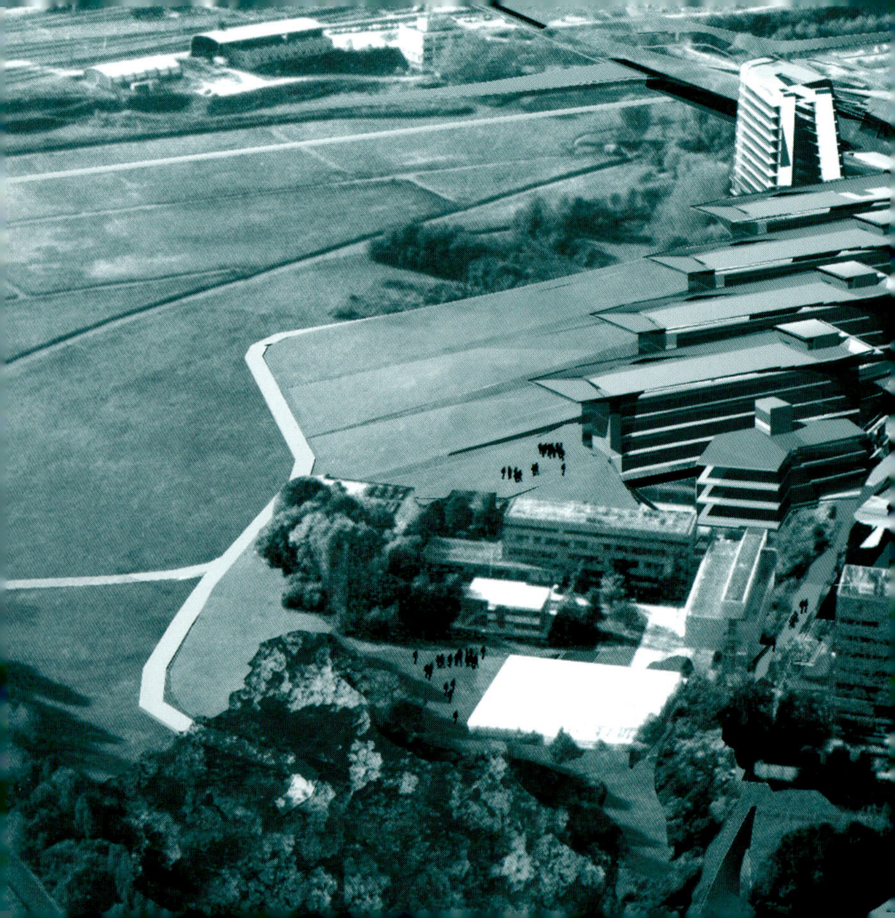

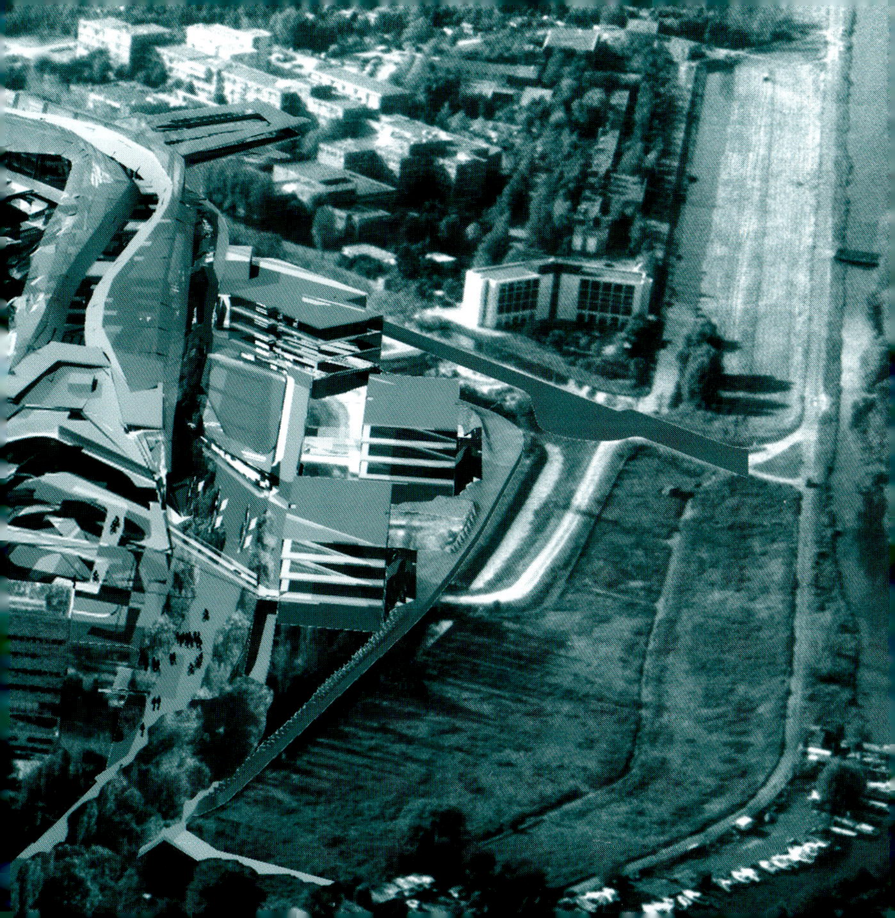

Eventual Masterplan

Legend:
1. FNWI Campus
2. Interactive concourse (at Level 2)
3. Commercial blocks (20-storeys)
4. Commercial blocks over Matrix buildings (20-storeys)
5. Apartment Blocks (max. 5-storeys)
6. FNWI Faculty Expansion
7. Institutional buildings
8. Departmental Store
9. Station Square
10. Train Complex
11. East-West link road from A10 motorway
12. Bicycle path
13. Congress
14. Hotel
15. Library
16. Eco-park
17. Marshland
18. Green House
19. Anna Hoeve Farmstead
20. Winterboom
21. Outdoor Sports Facilities

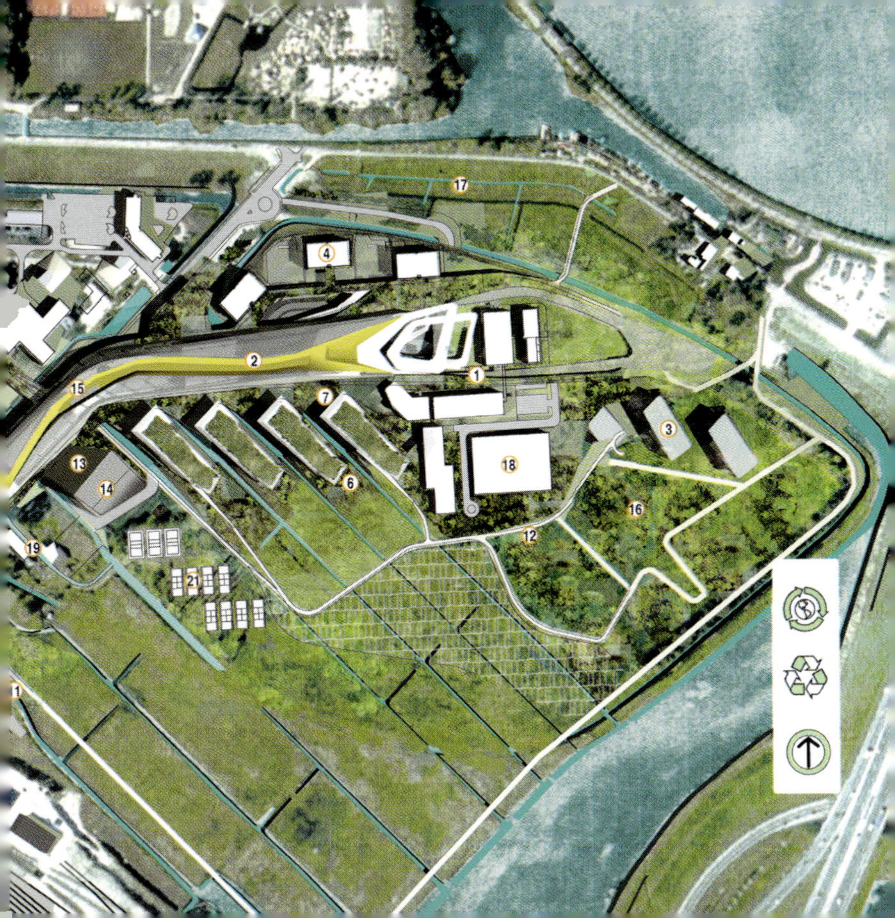
17
4
2
1
15
7
3
13
14
18
6
16
12
19
21
11

Level 1 (Car Parking) (-3.9m NAP)

a. Main drop-off
b. Entrance plaza
c. Ramp up to main entrance
d. Water feature
e. Loading dock
f. Distribution centre
g. Material recycling centre
h. Water recycling centre
i. Algae tank
j. Photovoltaic energy storage station
k. Electric buggy charging bank
l. Service core
m. Bus stop
n. Taxi stop
o. Car parking (700 bays)
p. Bicycle parking (2,500 bays)
q. Bus waiting (8 bays)
r. Truck bays (3 nos)

Key
- Offices
- (lecture) Halls, meeting areas
- Practice labs
- Laboratories
- Technical dept.
- Catering
- Warehouse/Storage
- Library
- Green houses
- Collections
- Sports and cultural facilities
- Hotel
- Congress areas
- Parking

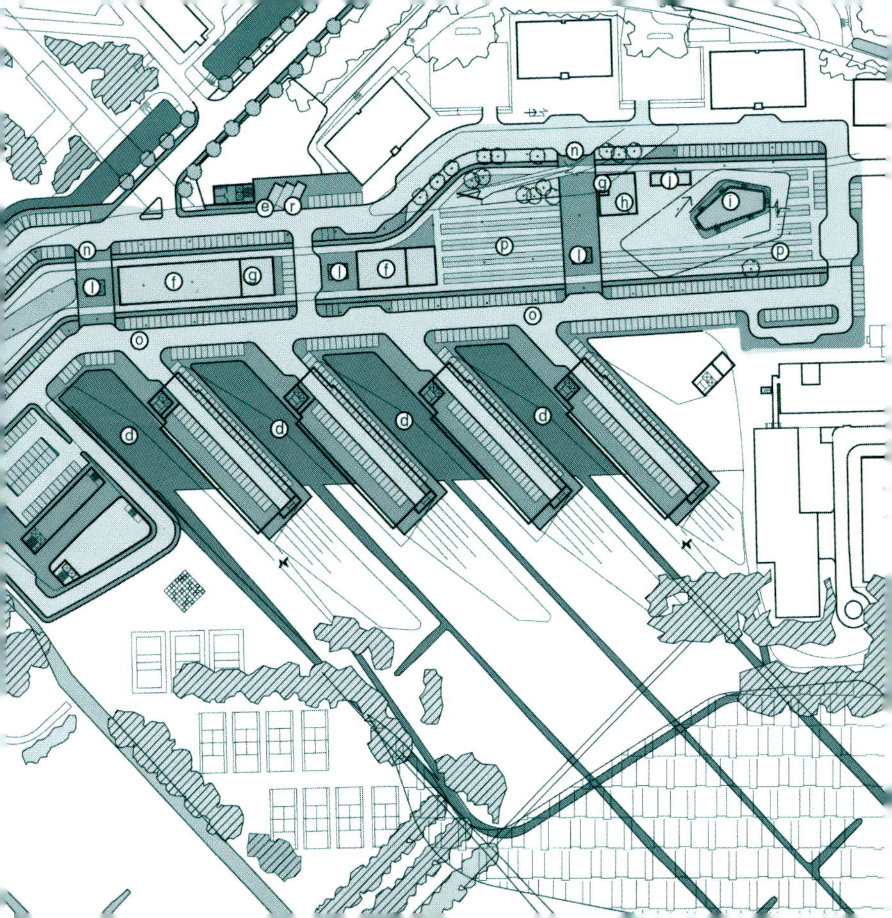

n
e
r
g
h
j
i
l
f
p
o
d

Level 2 (Main Concourse) (+1.6m NAP)

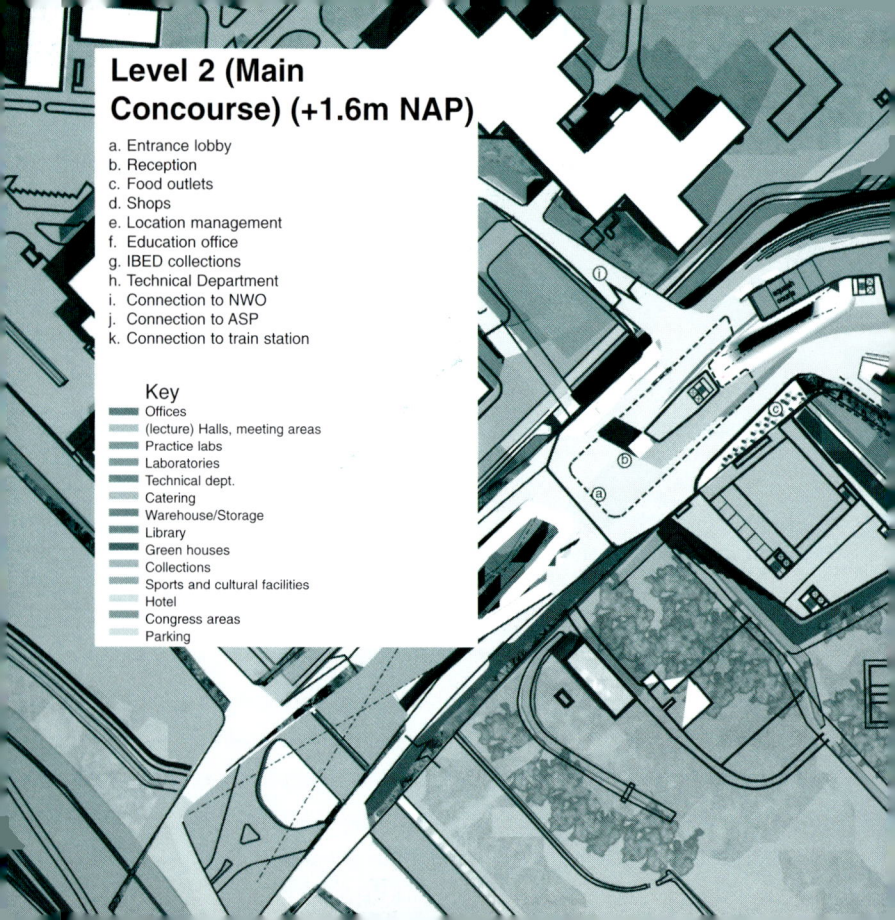

a. Entrance lobby
b. Reception
c. Food outlets
d. Shops
e. Location management
f. Education office
g. IBED collections
h. Technical Department
i. Connection to NWO
j. Connection to ASP
k. Connection to train station

Key
- Offices
- (lecture) Halls, meeting areas
- Practice labs
- Laboratories
- Technical dept.
- Catering
- Warehouse/Storage
- Library
- Green houses
- Collections
- Sports and cultural facilities
- Hotel
- Congress areas
- Parking

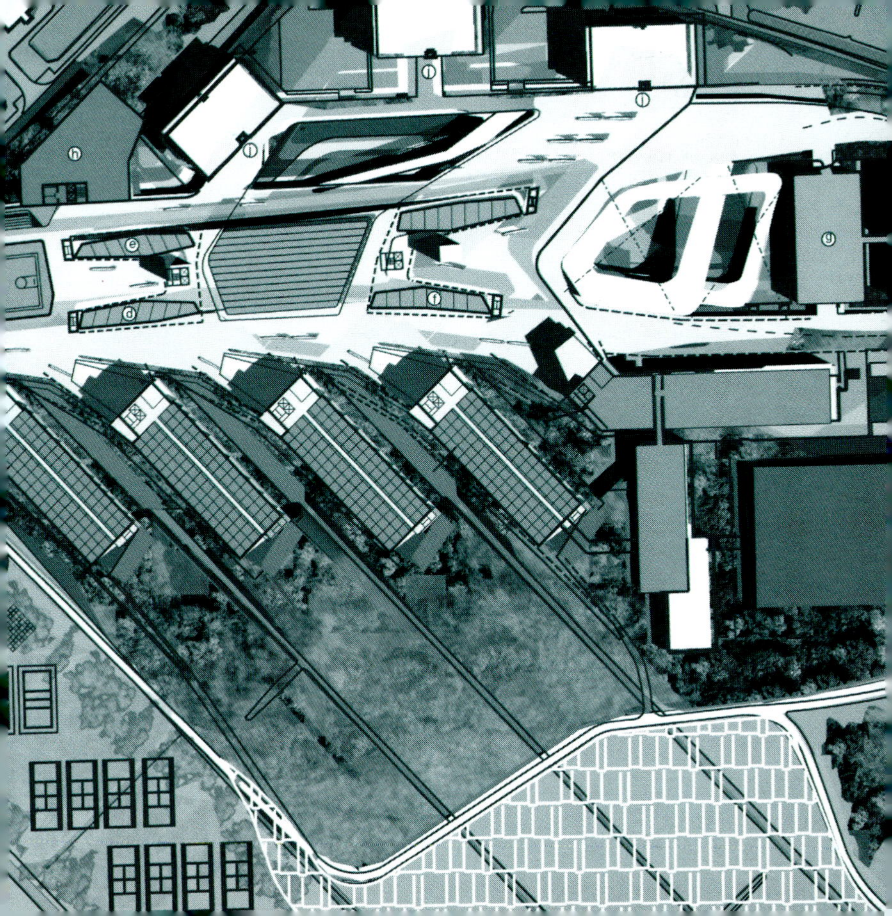
h
j
j
j
e
d
f
g

Level 1 (Car Parking)
(-3.9m NAP)

a. Laboratories
b. Green Belt with bicycle and footscooter path and pedestrian walkway
c. Education
d. Library
e. Media wall
f. Faculty offices

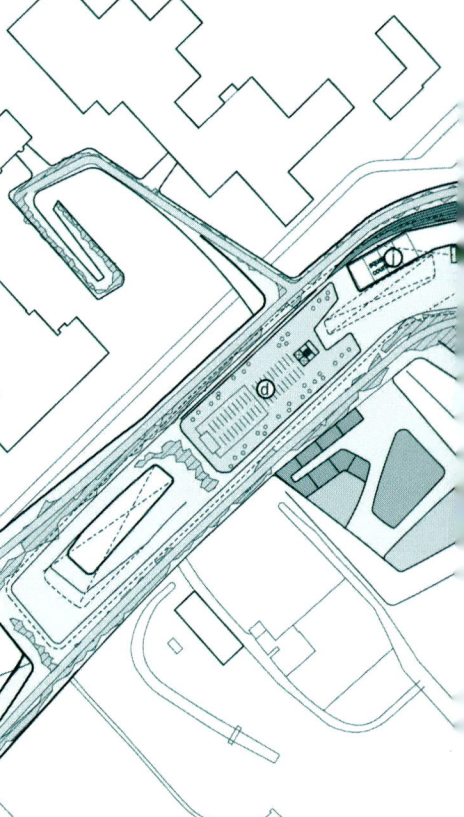

Key
- Offices
- (lecture) Halls, meeting areas
- Practice labs
- Laboratories
- Technical dept.
- Catering
- Warehouse/Storage
- Library
- Green houses
- Collections
- Sports and cultural facilities
- Hotel
- Congress areas
- Parking

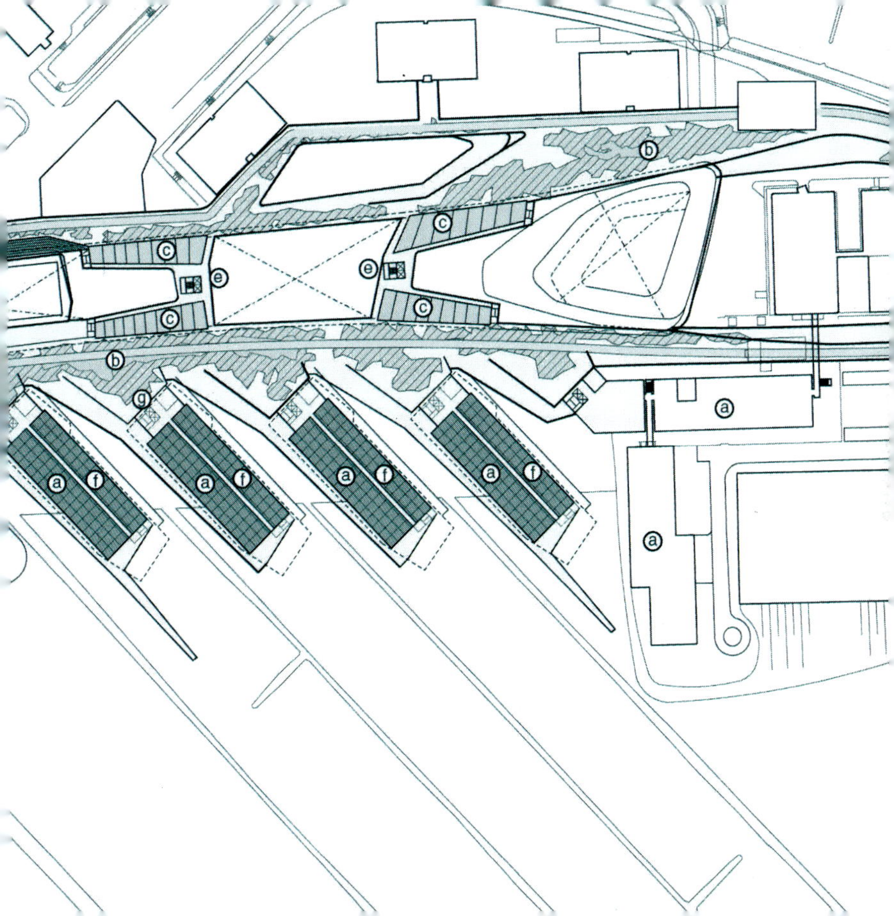
b
c
c
e
e
c
c
b
g
a
a
f
a
f
a
f
a
f
a

L4 & 5 (Typical) (+9.7 & +13.3m NAP)

a. Faculty offices
b. Education
c. Library

Key
- Offices
- (lecture) Halls, meeting areas
- Practice labs
- Laboratories
- Technical dept.
- Catering
- Warehouse/Storage
- Library
- Green houses
- Collections
- Sports and cultural facilities
- Hotel
- Congress areas
- Parking

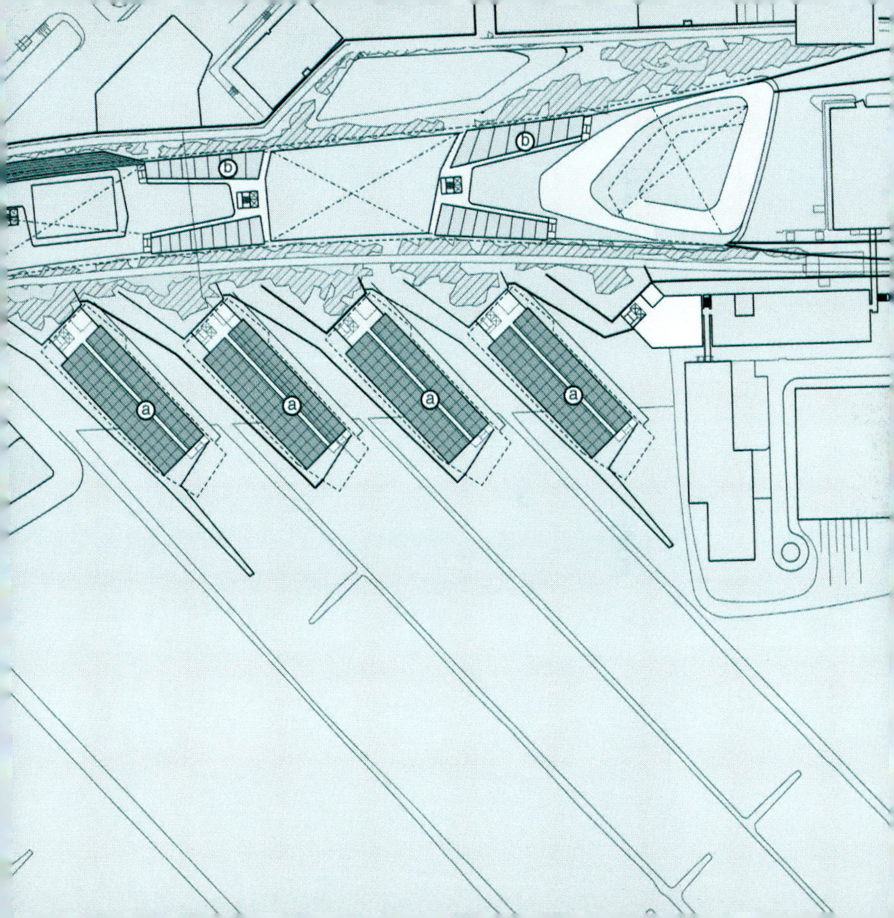
b
b
a
a
a
a

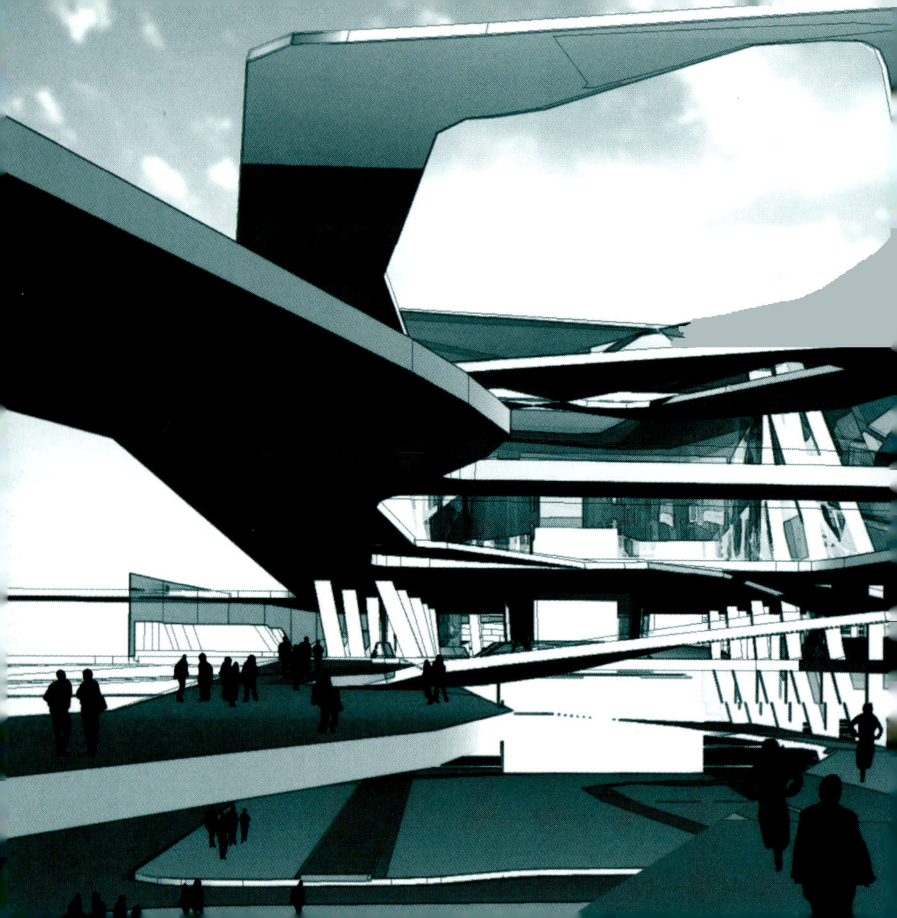

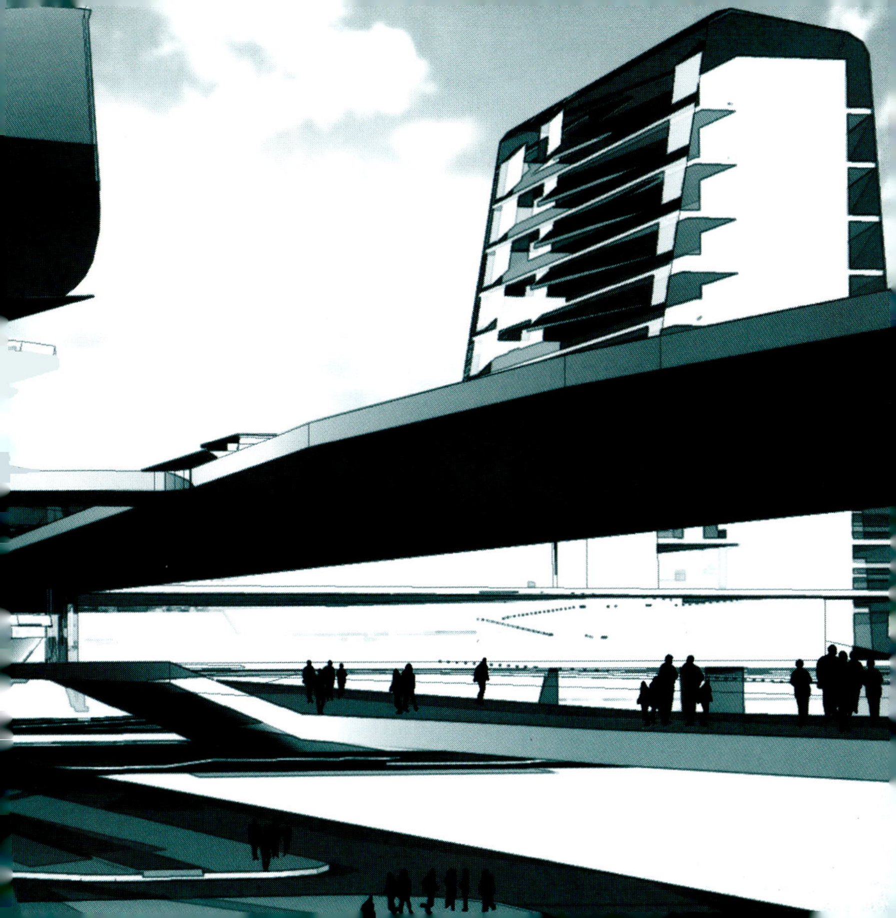

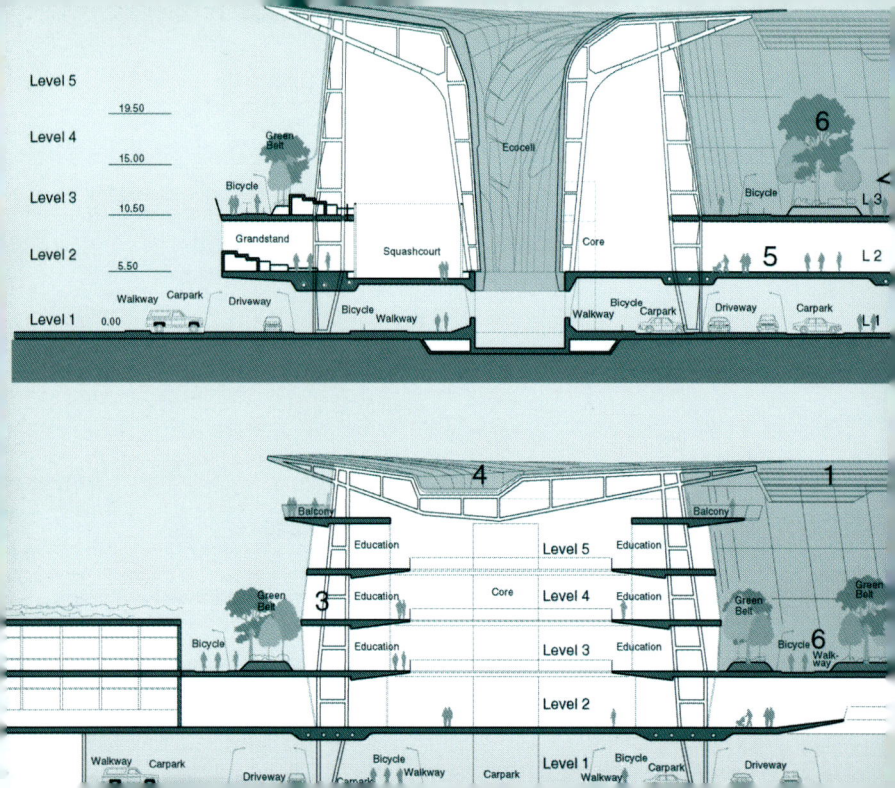

Level	Height
Level 5	19.50
Level 4	15.00
Level 3	10.50
Level 2	5.50
Level 1	0.00

Green Belt · Bicycle · Grandstand · Squashcourt · Ecocell · Core · Bicycle
Walkway · Carpark · Driveway · Bicycle · Walkway · Walkway · Bicycle · Carpark · Driveway · Carpark

Balcony · Education · Level 5 · Core · Level 4 · Level 3 · Level 2 · Green Belt · Walkway · Bicycle
Walkway · Carpark · Driveway · Bicycle · Walkway · Carpark · Level 1 · Bicycle · Walkway · Driveway

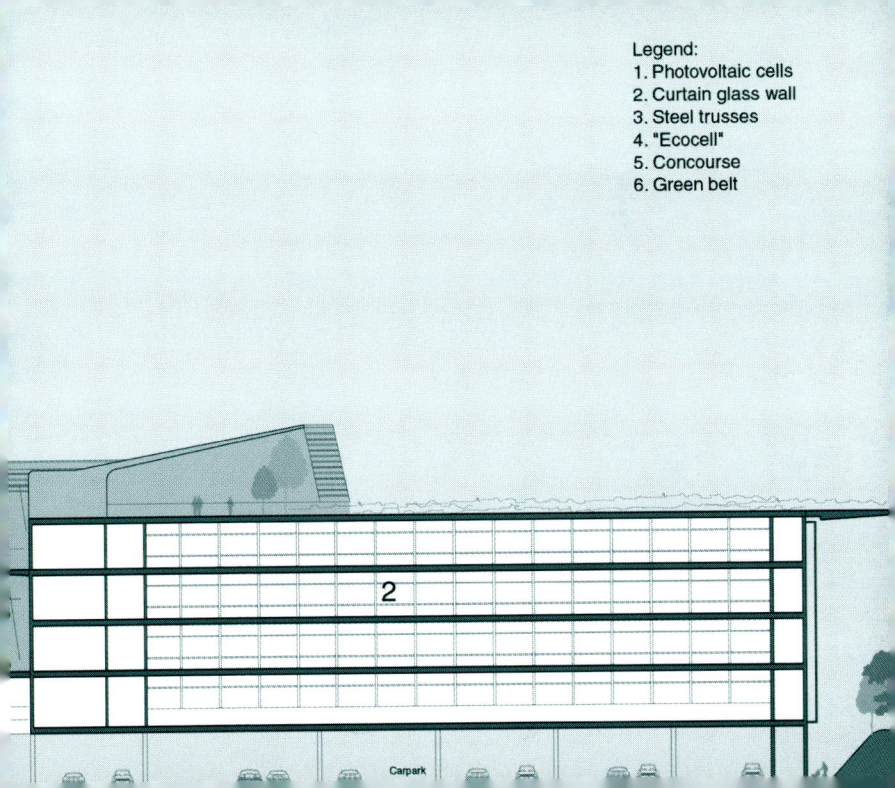

Legend:
1. Photovoltaic cells
2. Curtain glass wall
3. Steel trusses
4. "Ecocell"
5. Concourse
6. Green belt

2

Carpark

Legend:
1. Photovoltaic cells
2. Curtain glass wall
3. Louvered skylight
4. Precast Panels
5. Steel trusses
6. Structural steel frame
7. Congress
8. Hotel
9. Concourse
10. Library

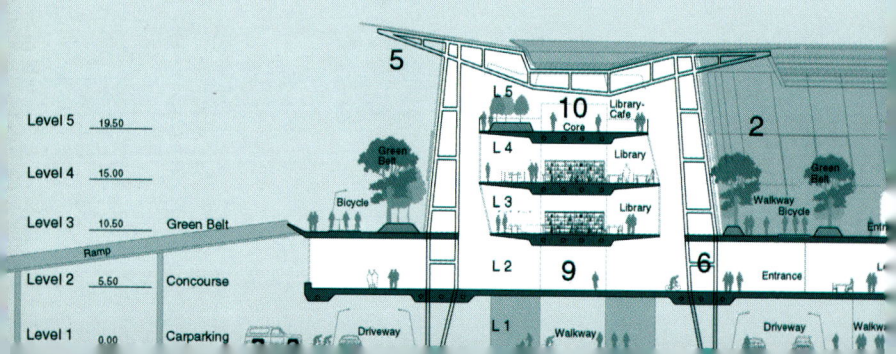

Level	Elevation	
Level 5	19.50	
Level 4	15.00	
Level 3	10.50	Green Belt
Level 2	5.50	Concourse
Level 1	0.00	Carparking

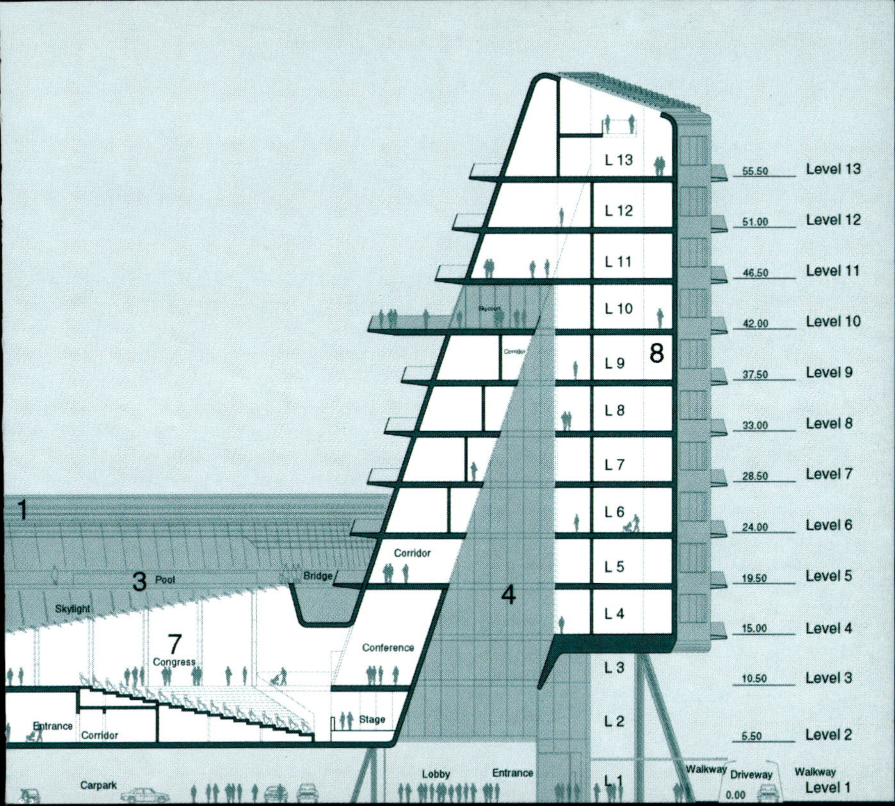

L 13
55.50
Level 13
L 12
51.00
Level 12
L 11
46.50
Level 11
L 10
42.00
Level 10
L 9
8
37.50
Level 9
L 8
33.00
Level 8
L 7
28.50
Level 7
1
L 6
24.00
Level 6
Corridor
3 Pool
Bridge
L 5
19.50
Level 5
Skylight
4
L 4
15.00
Level 4
7
Congress
Conference
L 3
10.50
Level 3
Entrance
Corridor
Stage
L 2
5.50
Level 2
Carpark
Lobby
Entrance
L 1
Walkway
Driveway
Walkway
0.00
Level 1

ecocells 106

South Elevation

ecocells 107

West Elevation

ecocells 108

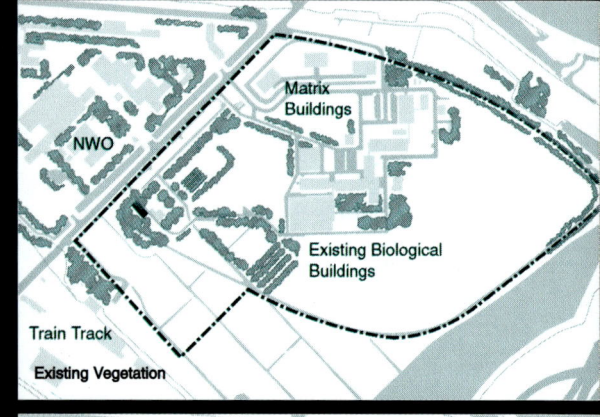

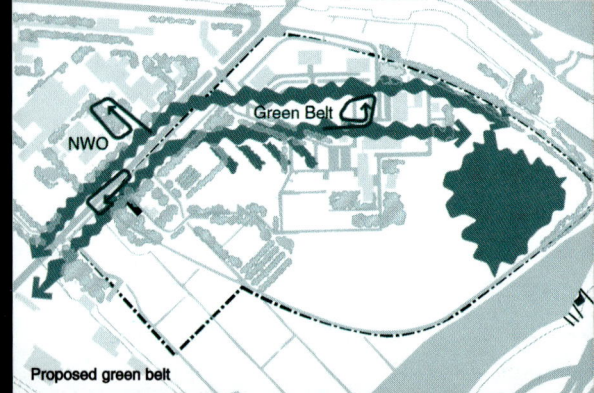

Other buildings

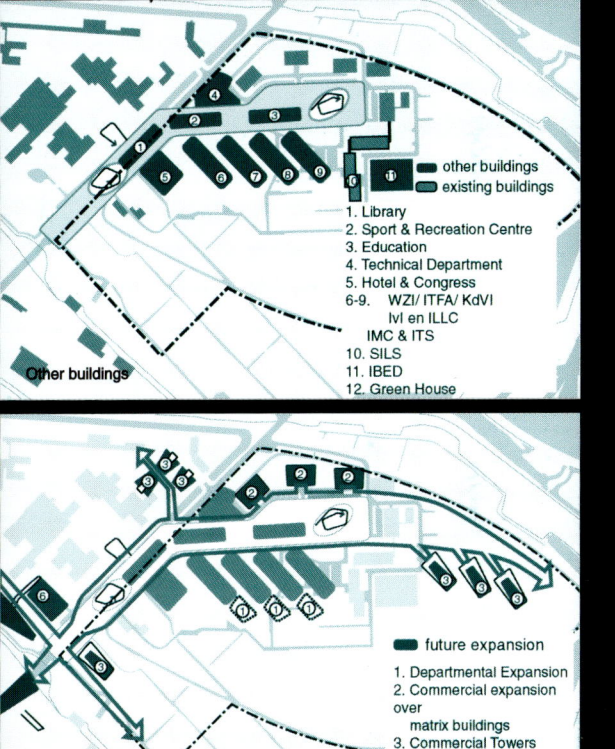

1. Library
2. Sport & Recreation Centre
3. Education
4. Technical Department
5. Hotel & Congress
6-9. WZI/ ITFA/ KdVI
   lvl en ILLC
   IMC & ITS
10. SILS
11. IBED
12. Green House

Future development

future expansion

1. Departmental Expansion
2. Commercial expansion over matrix buildings
3. Commercial Towers
4. Train Station
5. Hypermarket and
6. Department Store

ecocells 109

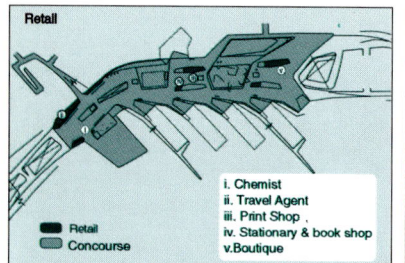

Retail

- i. Chemist
- ii. Travel Agent
- iii. Print Shop
- iv. Stationary & book shop
- v. Boutique

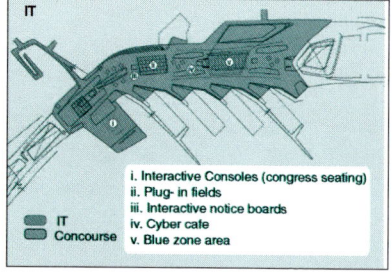

Legend: Retail / Concourse

IT

- i. Interactive Consoles (congress seating)
- ii. Plug-in fields
- iii. Interactive notice boards
- iv. Cyber cafe
- v. Blue zone area

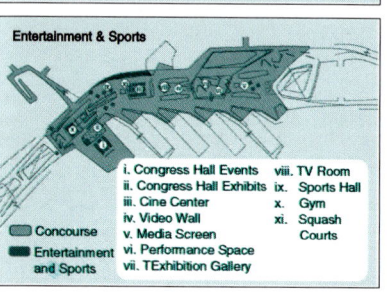

Legend: IT / Concourse

Entertainment & Sports

- i. Congress Hall Events
- ii. Congress Hall Exhibits
- iii. Cine Center
- iv. Video Wall
- v. Media Screen
- vi. Performance Space
- vii. TExhibition Gallery
- viii. TV Room
- ix. Sports Hall
- x. Gym
- xi. Squash Courts

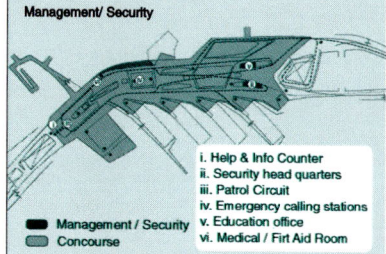

Legend: Concourse / Entertainment and Sports

Management/ Security

- i. Help & Info Counter
- ii. Security head quarters
- iii. Patrol Circuit
- iv. Emergency calling stations
- v. Education office
- vi. Medical / First Aid Room

Legend: Management / Security / Concourse

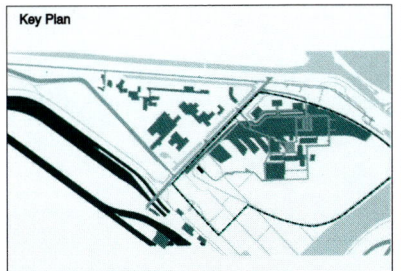

Key Plan

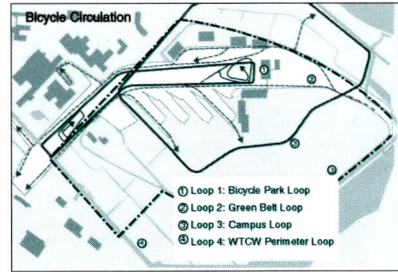

Bicycle Circulation
① Loop 1: Bicycle Park Loop
② Loop 2: Green Belt Loop
③ Loop 3: Campus Loop
④ Loop 4: WTCW Perimeter Loop

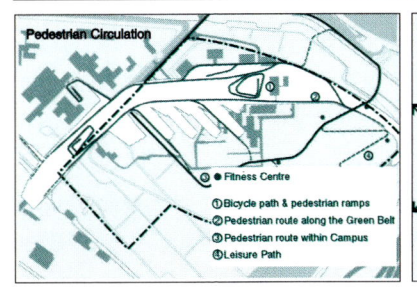

Pedestrian Circulation
● Fitness Centre
① Bicycle path & pedestrian ramps
② Pedestrian route along the Green Belt
③ Pedestrian route within Campus
④ Leisure Path

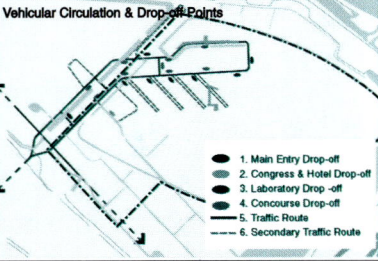

Vehicular Circulation & Drop-off Points
1. Main Entry Drop-off
2. Congress & Hotel Drop-off
3. Laboratory Drop-off
4. Concourse Drop-off
5. Traffic Route
6. Secondary Traffic Route

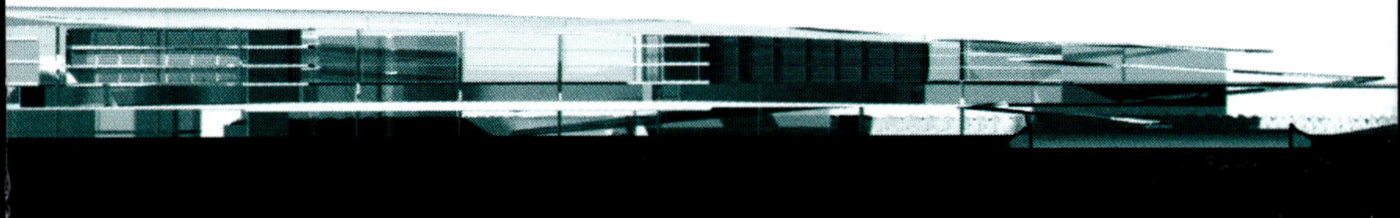

ecocells

Phase 1

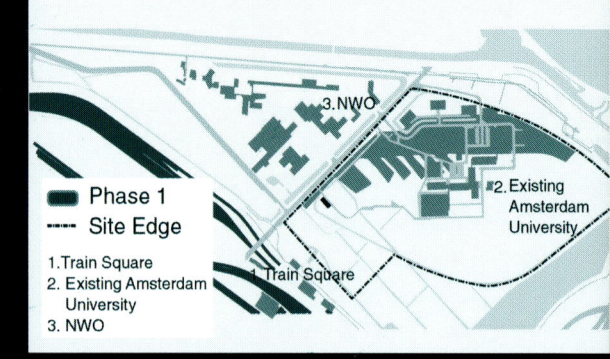

- Phase 1
- Site Edge
1. Train Square
2. Existing Amsterdam University
3. NWO

Phase 1b

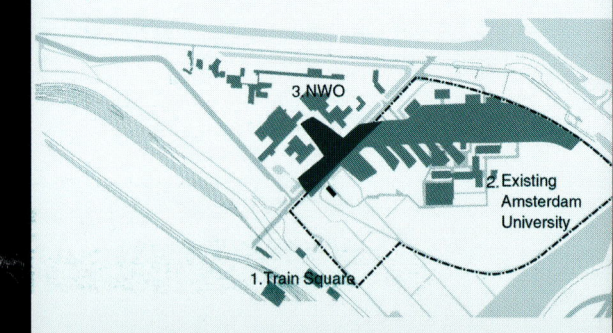

Phase 2

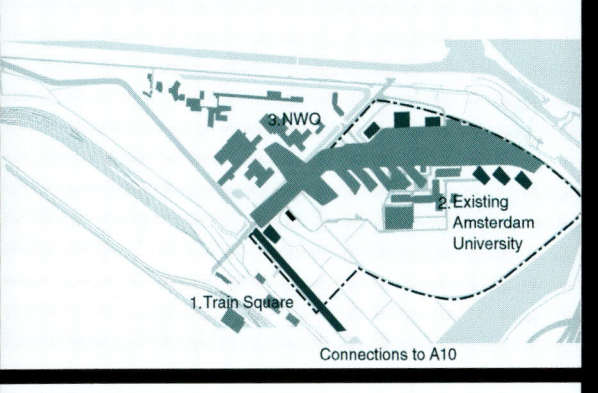

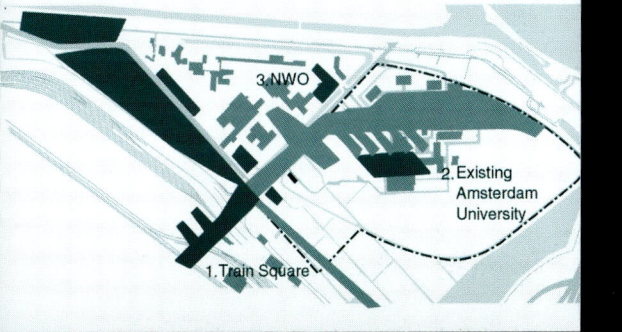

3. NWO
2. Existing Amsterdam University
1. Train Square
Connections to A10

Future Phases

3. NWO
2. Existing Amsterdam University
1. Train Square

ecocells 113

ecocells 114

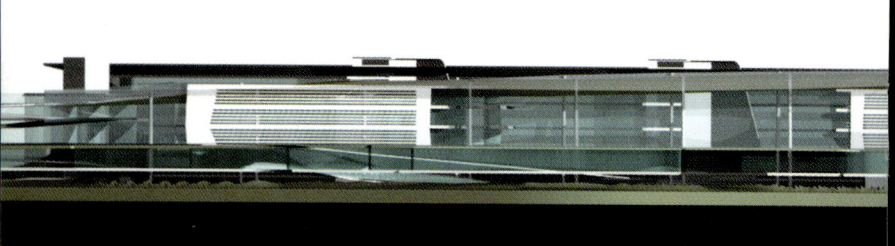

East Elevation

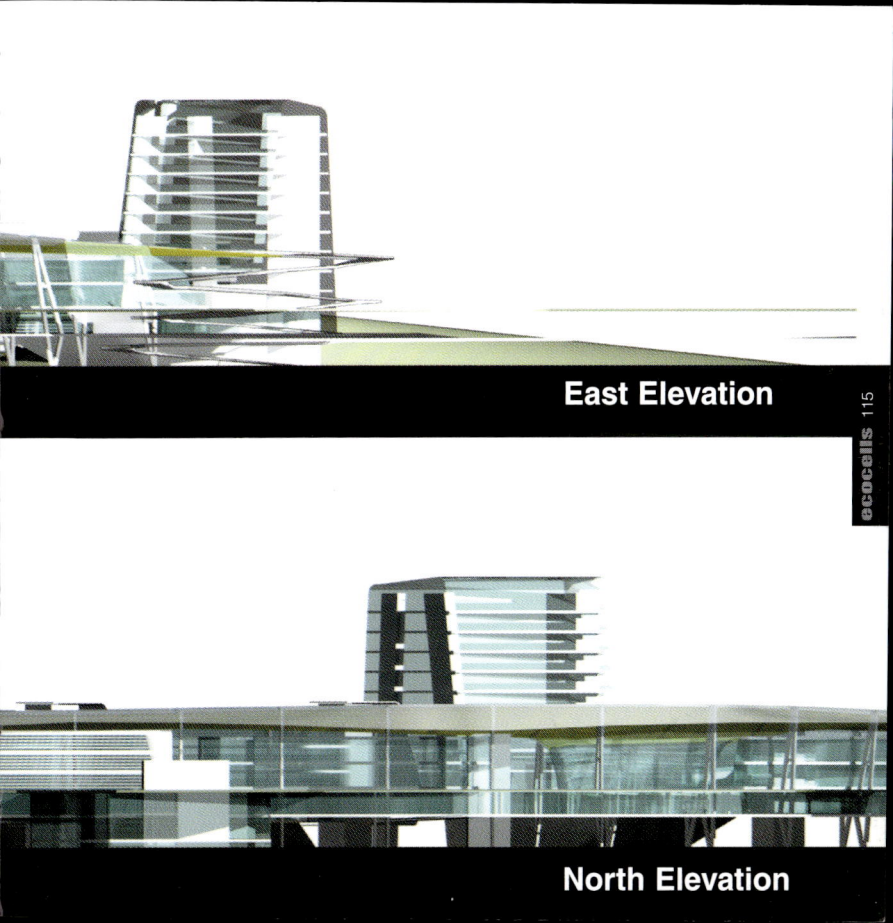

ecocells 115

North Elevation

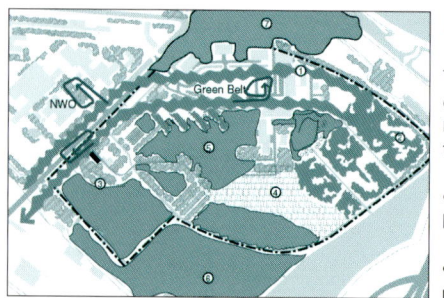

Landscape Strategy

The landscape is designed to reflect the cultural and ecological character of the locality. The landscape design has the following aims:

• To maintain and enhance the landscape assets of the site.

• To provide for outdoor active recreational and other functions as developed in the brief subject to discussion with the faculty.

• To provide for passive recreation in order to promote the health of all faculty members and visitors.

• To contribute to the City of Amsterdan's ecological policies and Agenda 21 policies.

• To promote species diversity, biomass, and wildlife by creation of a series of polder landscape effects.

• To provide outdoor visual amenity and beauty.

• To provide visual relief most especially in order to change eye focus for those using computer screens.

• To "remember" the history of the site.

• To deal with surface water and roof drainage on site (by directly running it into the pools as necessary with reed treatment).

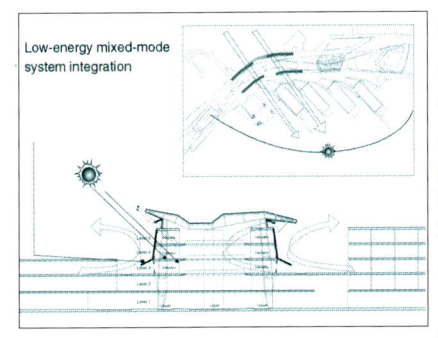

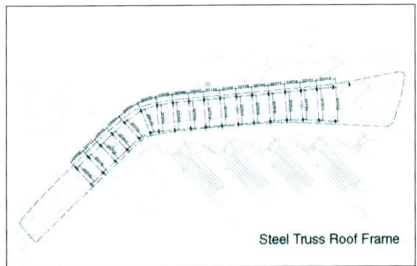

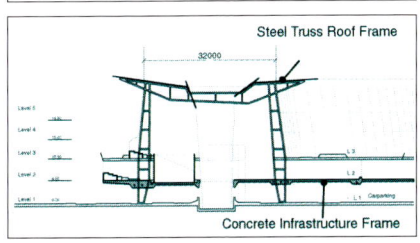

Mechanical Integration

The scheme has integrated mixed-mode and low energy systems.

The scheme is designed as a low-energy building using mixed-mode cooling/heating and low energy mechanical and electrical systems, where possible. The targeted overall building energy consumption should be within 170kWh/sqm/annum.

Supplementary energy is provided by the use of photovoltaic cells on the roof level.

Structural Concept

The buildings are constructed in steel with a reinforced concrete infrastructure frame.

The basic infrastructure frame in reinforced concrete encompasses the Level 2 concourse floor plate and columns, and the main service cores. The remaining structures are in steel-frame construction.

The concourse roof is constructed in steel trusses providing for a column-free span over the concourse. The trusses support a moulded trough that collects rainwater and channels it into the "ecocells".

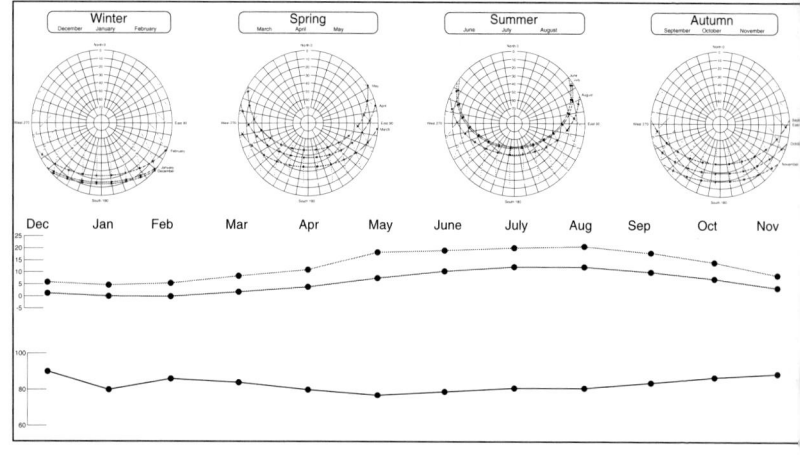

Bioclimatic Responses

The buildings are designed as low energy buildings.

Bioclimatic responses involve use of passive and mixed-mode means to maintain internal comfort levels. Illustrated here is the use of wind hatches as "environmental modifiers".

The wind hatches scoops in wind in summer to cool the concourse, closes in winter to trap heat, and uses adjustable openings during mid-seasons to get the right amount of cooling depending on the external weather conditions.

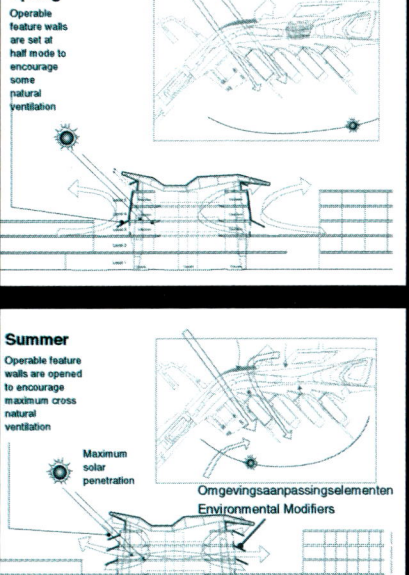

Spring
Operable feature walls are set at half mode to encourage some natural ventilation

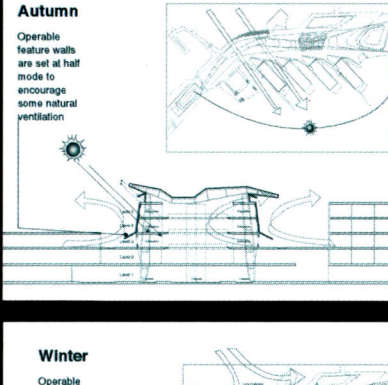

Autumn
Operable feature walls are set at half mode to encourage some natural ventilation

Summer
Operable feature walls are opened to encourage maximum cross natural ventilation

Maximum solar penetration

Omgevingsaanpassingselementen
Environmental Modifiers

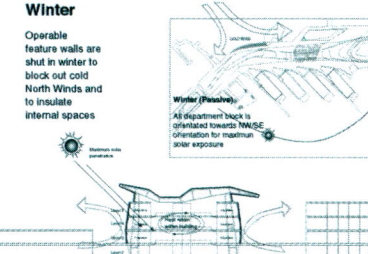

Winter
Operable feature walls are shut in winter to block out cold North Winds and to insulate internal spaces

Winter (Passive)
All department block is orientated towards NW/SE orientation for maximum solar exposure

Flow Diagrams

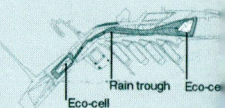

Water Flow

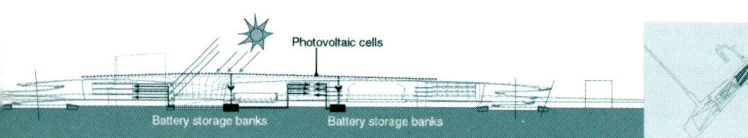

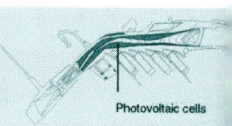

- Water tank
- Roof trough for rain water collection
- Water collection
- Water recycling centre
- Eco-cell
- Rain trough
- Eco-cell

Energy Flow

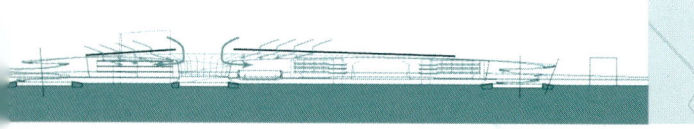

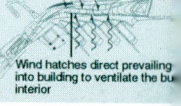

- Photovoltaic cells
- Battery storage banks
- Battery storage banks
- Photovoltaic cells

Wind Flow

- Wind hatches direct prevailing into building to ventilate the building interior

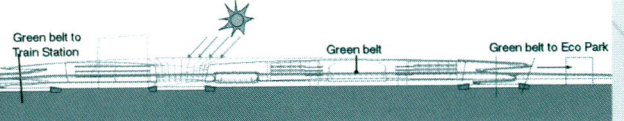

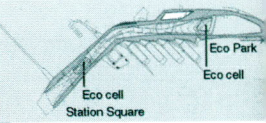

Vegetation Flow

- Green belt to Train Station
- Green belt
- Green belt to Eco Park
- Eco cell
- Station Square
- Eco Park
- Eco cell

Material Flow

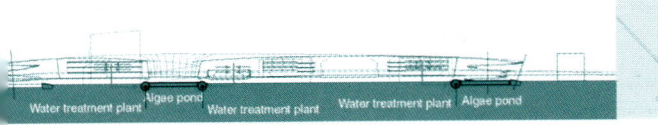

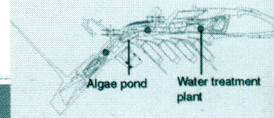

- Material recycling chute
- Recycling Centre
- Distribution Centre
- Distribution Centre
- Recycling Centre

Sewage Flow

- Water treatment plant
- Algae pond

Bio-Climatic Responses

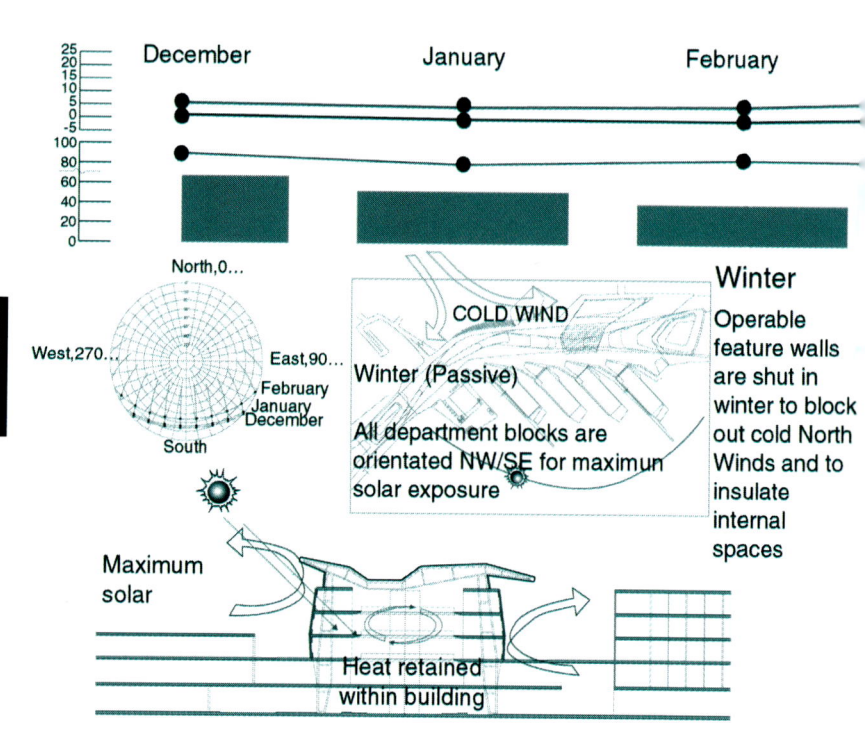

December | January | February

North, 0...
West, 270...
East, 90...
February
January
December
South

Winter

COLD WIND

Winter (Passive)

All department blocks are orientated NW/SE for maximum solar exposure

Operable feature walls are shut in winter to block out cold North Winds and to insulate internal spaces

Maximum solar

Heat retained within building

ecocells 122

| March | April | May |

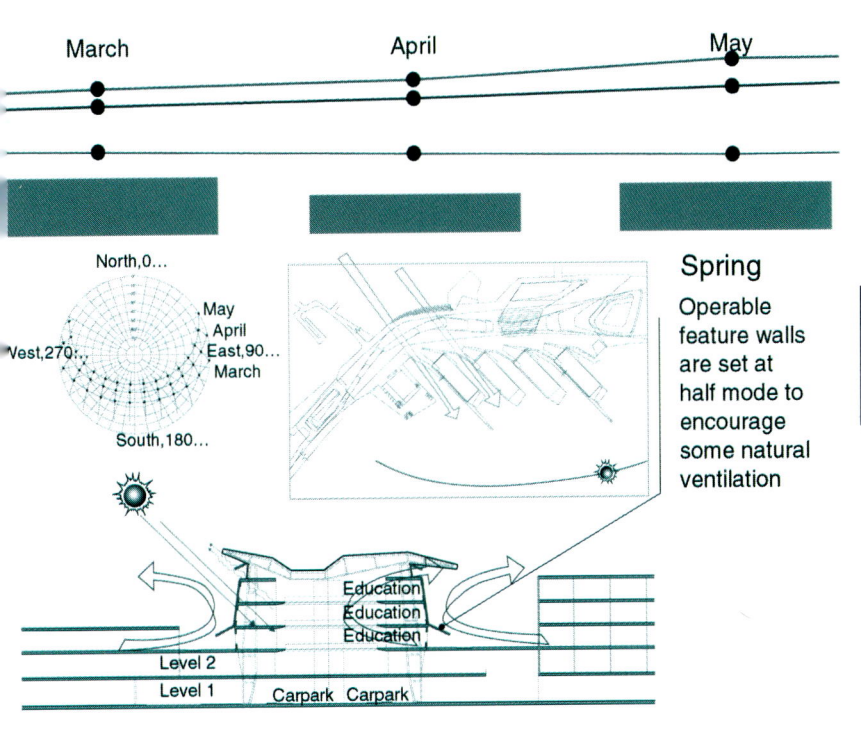

North, 0...
May
April
West, 270... East, 90...
March
South, 180...

Spring

Operable feature walls are set at half mode to encourage some natural ventilation

Education
Education
Education
Level 2
Level 1   Carpark   Carpark

ecocells

June | July | August

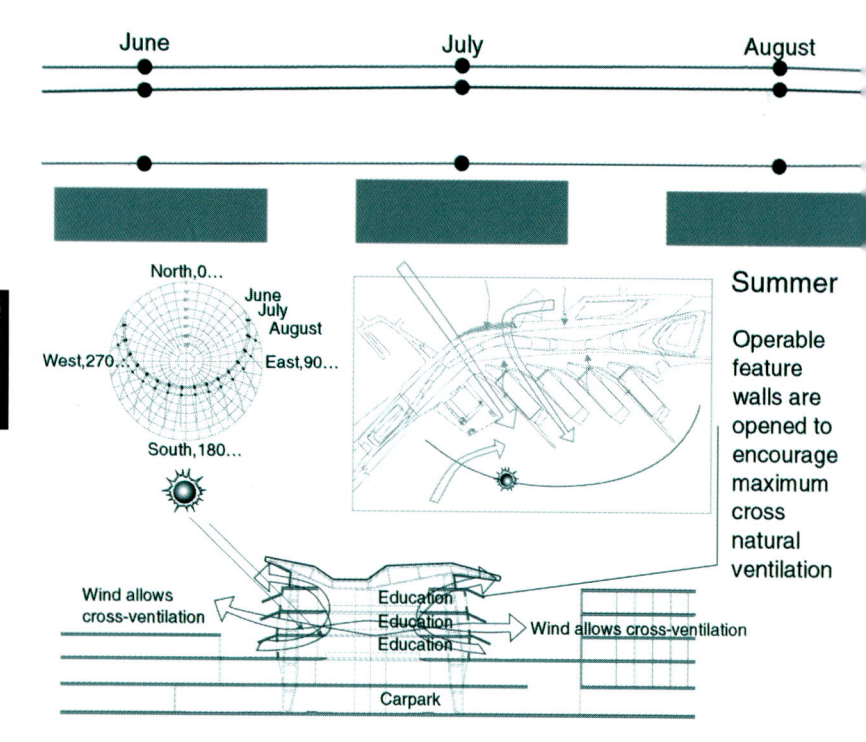

North, 0...
June
July
August
West, 270... East, 90...
South, 180...

Summer

Operable feature walls are opened to encourage maximum cross natural ventilation

Wind allows cross-ventilation — Education / Education / Education — Wind allows cross-ventilation

Carpark

September   October   November

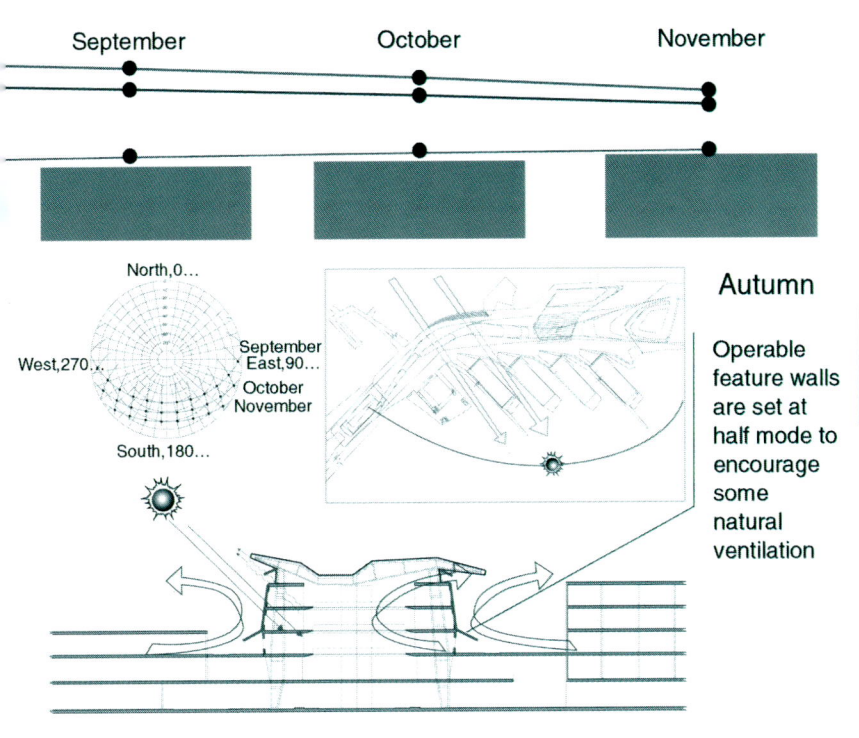

North, 0...
West, 270...
September East, 90...
October
November
South, 180...

Autumn

Operable feature walls are set at half mode to encourage some natural ventilation

ecocells 125

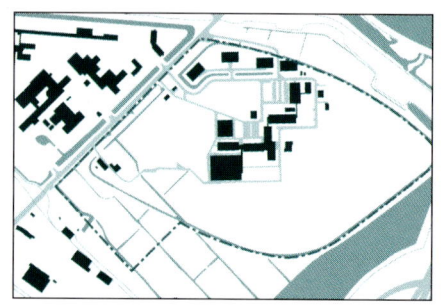

Existing Figure Ground

The scheme unifies the existing buildings by filling up the negative spaces between buildings to create an efficient and compact development

The existing buildings are in disparate locations, spread-out over the WTCW area.

The existing figure ground lacks any clear form of organisation.

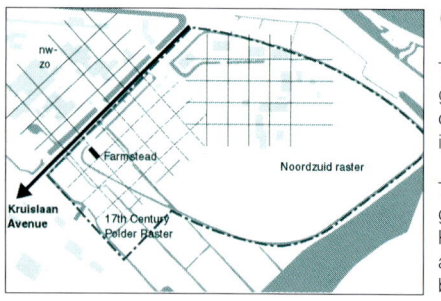

Organisational Grids

The scheme assimilates the 2 existing grids into a unified composition without creating awkward conditions at the grid intersections.

There are 2 existing organisational grids: The buildings to the West of Kruislaan follow a NW-SE grid that aligns to the original polder grid, while buildings to the East of Kruislaan follow a N-S grid.

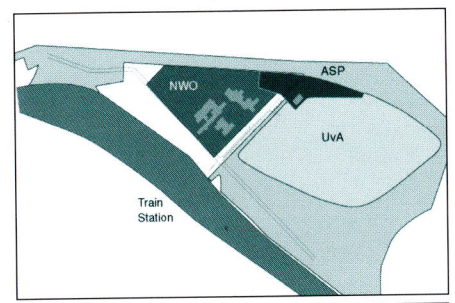

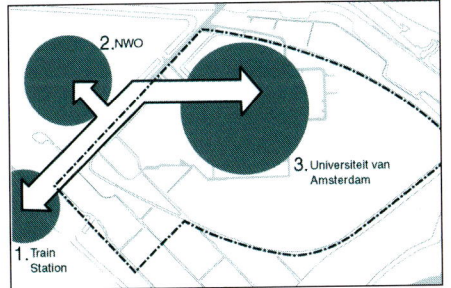

Users of the Facilities

The scheme provides the opportunity for the main users of the facilities to be more closely integrated and to interact socially and communally by sharing common facilities spread out at Level 2 as a concourse.

The WTCW site has 3 main institutions: NWO, Amsterdam Science Park (ASP), and the University of Amsterdam (UvA). The railway station at the Kruislaan and railway line intersection serves these institutions.

Essential Linkages

The scheme improves connections between the station and the institutions by providing the shortest possible route linking all buildings and taking into account safety and weather protection. A large portion of people arriving to the WTCW arrive by train, making pedestrian linkage between the train station, NWO and UvA / ASP an important consideration.

Currently poor pedestrian connections exist between the 3 institutions and the train station. To get to the institutes from the station, the commuter will need to walk 250m to NWO and 700m to the Biology Block of UvA in non-protected weather conditions.

The essential linkage is identified here as one that connects all 3 institutions to the train station, that starts from the Train Square, goes along Kruislaan till the NWO entrance before branching eastwards toward the ASP/UvA group of buildings.

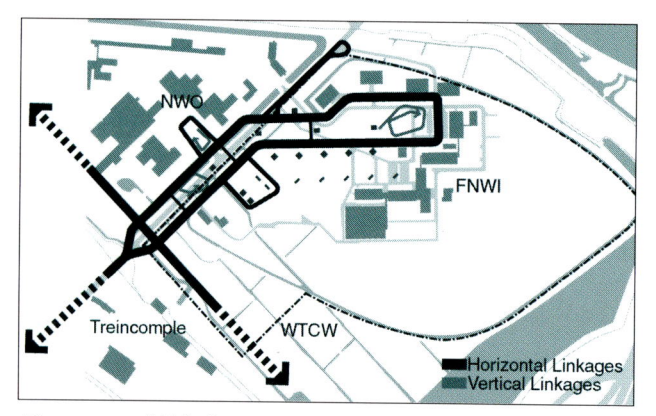

Proposed Linkages at Level 1 (-3.9m NAP)

Essentially Level 1 is the vehicular circulation level (for buses, vehicular access, drop-offs etc.).

It is proposed that vehicular traffic, cyclists and pedestrian traffic be given separate paths within the existing linkage route. Level 1 which is the existing street level should be predominantly designated for vehicular traffic.

At the point of arrival immediately after the station tunnel, the road bifurcates to the East and West of the Kruislaan, freeing up the median strip for development of an interaction strip. Within this interaction strip on Level 1 are vertical linkages to the upper floors, which include ramps, stairs and lift cores.

Secondary access roads into the FNWI campus, NWO and ASP tees off from the main circulation loop on either sides of the Kruislaan.

Off-street parking is provided around the circulation loop.

Proposed Interaction Zone at Level 2 (+1.6m NAP)

The concourse is the main feature of the scheme as an interaction zone and makes the scheme unique.

Provided within the Level 2 Interaction Zone is a concourse, which would house shared facilities for FNWI and the buildings within the WTCW area.

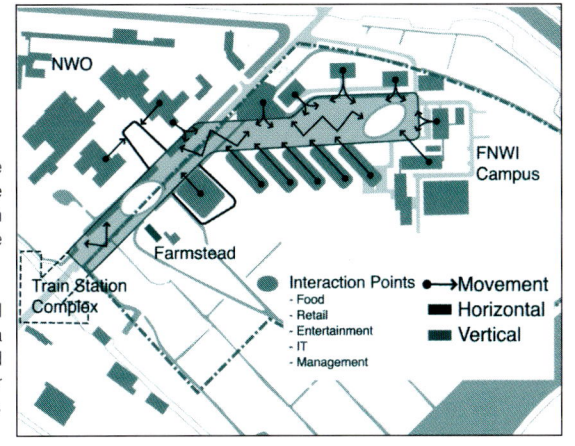

Interaction Points — Movement
- Food
- Retail
- Entertainment
- IT
- Management

Horizontal
Vertical

The concourse is raised above dike level (to give views to the waterways) and is at the same level as the future train station complex, providing a direct connection into the station. It is proposed that the concourse be the new entry datum level to the FNWI buildings and eventually to which all buildings shall be connected to within the WTCW planning area.

As an interaction zone, the concourse will contain a palette of key facilities and cultural activities, including food outlets, retail, entertainment and IT hubs catering to the users.

The concourse will be "highly-wired" enabling users to connect into the information grid of the scientific institutions within the WTCW. Possible IT features within the concourse would be a "Blue Zone" area, which utilises wireless technology, media screen walls, interactive touch screens, and IT poles where students/users may plug in their laptops to download information.

Education

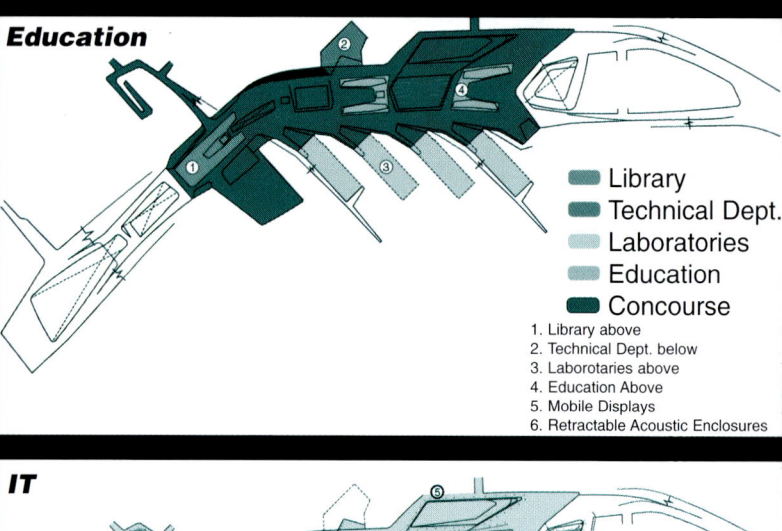

- Library
- Technical Dept.
- Laboratories
- Education
- Concourse

1. Library above
2. Technical Dept. below
3. Laborataries above
4. Education Above
5. Mobile Displays
6. Retractable Acoustic Enclosures

IT

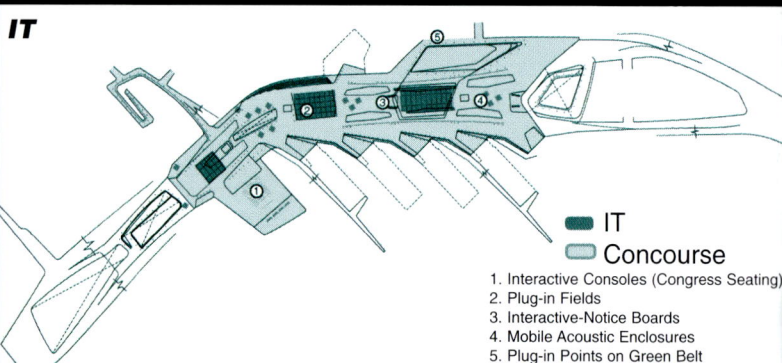

- IT
- Concourse

1. Interactive Consoles (Congress Seating)
2. Plug-in Fields
3. Interactive-Notice Boards
4. Mobile Acoustic Enclosures
5. Plug-in Points on Green Belt

Food

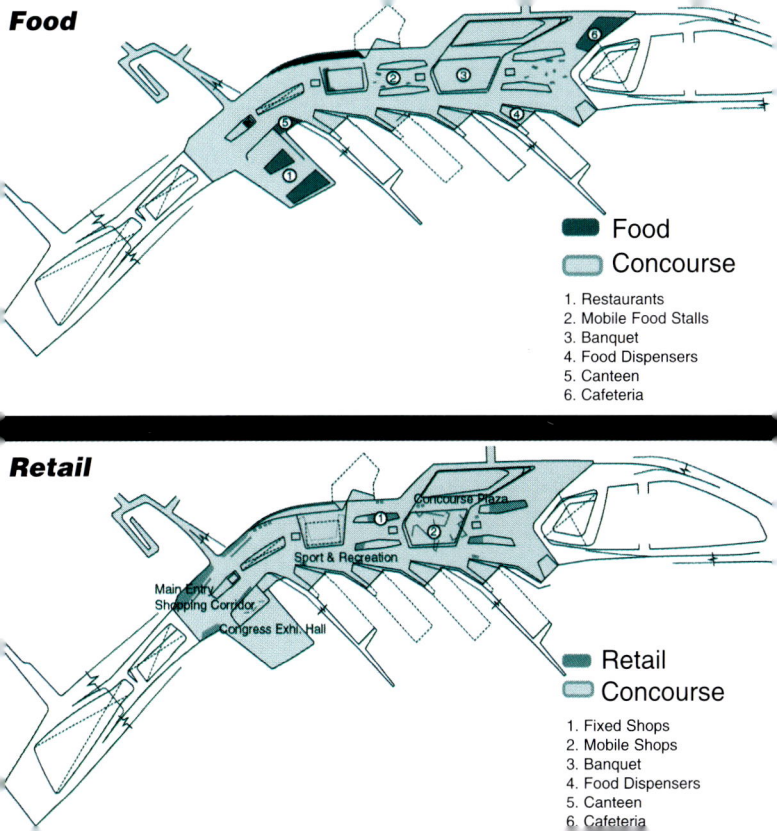

- Food
- Concourse

1. Restaurants
2. Mobile Food Stalls
3. Banquet
4. Food Dispensers
5. Canteen
6. Cafeteria

Retail

Concourse Plaza
Sport & Recreation
Main Entry
Shopping Corridor
Congress Exhi. Hall

- Retail
- Concourse

1. Fixed Shops
2. Mobile Shops
3. Banquet
4. Food Dispensers
5. Canteen
6. Cafeteria

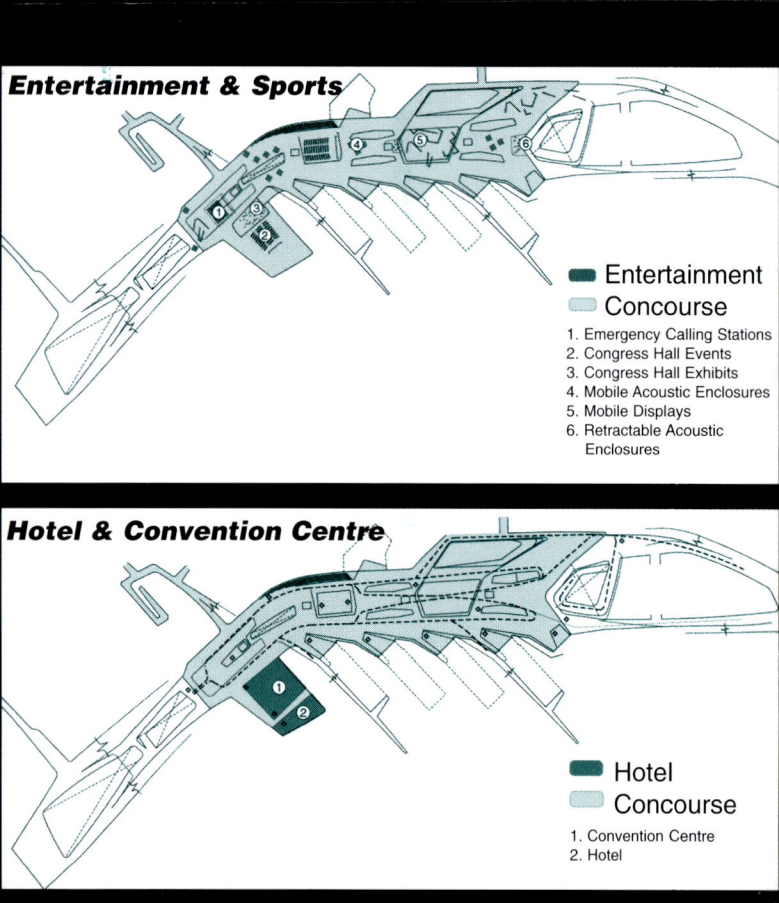

Entertainment & Sports

■ Entertainment
▢ Concourse

1. Emergency Calling Stations
2. Congress Hall Events
3. Congress Hall Exhibits
4. Mobile Acoustic Enclosures
5. Mobile Displays
6. Retractable Acoustic Enclosures

Hotel & Convention Centre

■ Hotel
▢ Concourse

1. Convention Centre
2. Hotel

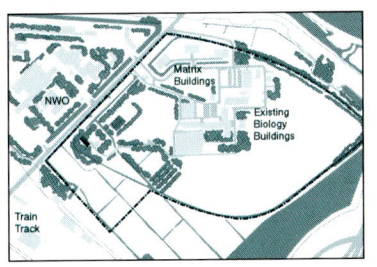

Existing Vegetation

The scheme retains (and at the same time enhances) the landscape of the site by minimising the building's footprint on the ground as well as the infrastructure, avoiding destruction of the existing ecological structure. Existing trees are mainly maintained (located in groups between buildings, which are more densely built-up to the west of Kruislaan). Much of the land on eastern parts of the site is maintained as green, with its established eco-system (i.e. fauna and flora, habitats, small animals nesting places etc.).

- Dense planting surrounds the existing Anna Houvre Farmhouse area.
- The landscape pattern on the N-W and South follows the original polder grid whereas those to the N-E are orthogonal following the grid of the UvA Biology block buildings.

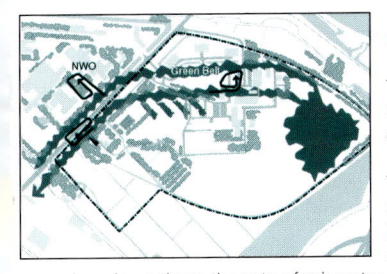

Proposed Green Belt at L3

The scheme increases the site's biomass by introducing rooftop vegetation which will also collect rainwater.

To replenish the loss biomass of large-scale developments, our scheme has a green belt on Level 3 above the concourse and the greening of the departmental block roofs. The roof greening slows down the rate of rainwater discharge into the ground.

Note: Large-scale developments result in a loss of the site's biomass, by removal of the site's existing vegetation and ground cover and replacement with buildings, which are primarily inorganic.

The green belt in this scheme leads to an ecological park on the east as a continuous green ecosystem enabling species migration, thus engendering a more stable ecosystem.

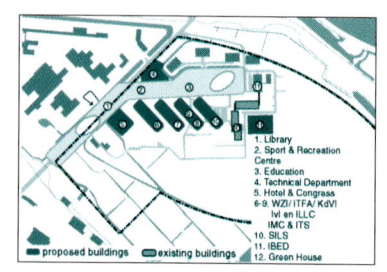

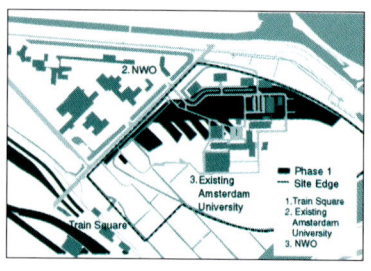

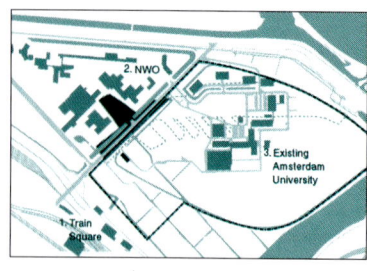

Linkages to other buildings

Our scheme enables other buildings to connect to the Concourse (at Level 2).

The concourse provides a platform for interaction between FNWI and the various institutions and departments within the WTCW, in line with the Client's vision of providing a stimulating scientific environment in this Centre for Science and Technology.

The central location of the concourse on the Kruislaan itself ensures easy accessibility to it by all users and makes this an obvious position for the location of the interactive zone.

Phasing

Phase 1
The total gross area for Phase 1 will be 76,000 sqm of new gross floor space and 16,000 sqm of renovation for the existing buildings (totalling 92,000 sqm).

The extent of Phase 1 construction will be as per the requirements of the FNWI design brief.

The design is essentially a concourse with "plugged-in" buildings.

While the departments are within the FNWI site boundaries, part of the concourse straddles over the Kruislaan. The concourse construction may be sub-phased into Phases 1a and 1b, to enable negotiation to sort out land matters while Phase 1a is under construction.

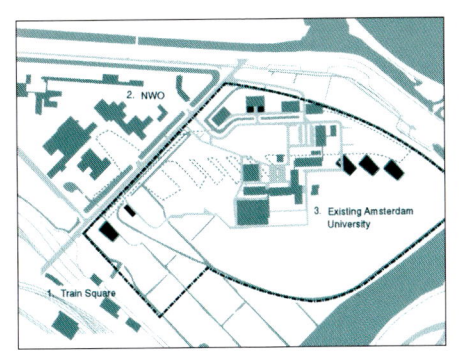

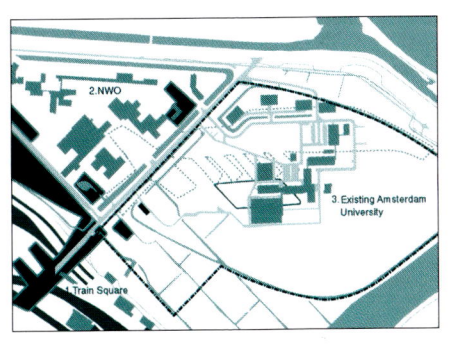

The total additional gross floor area for Phase 2 will be 190,000 sqm.
Phase 2 includes the remaining built-up areas for the sites east of Kruislaan to maximise the given plot ratio of 1.3 and will involve:
• Extension of the concourse to the east which will require the relocation of the existing Biology block (9,000 sqm).
• Expansion of existing departmental blocks (approx. 5,000 sqm).
• Addition of 3 new tower blocks plugged into the extended concourse, totalling 90,000 sqm.
• Building above the 3 existing Matrix buildings, yielding an additional 73,800 sqm.
• A new tower at the east-west road / Kruislaan intersection (30,000 sqm).

Future Phases

Each of the future phases will have provision for a direct covered-link to the concourse.

Future proposed developments to the west side of Kruislaan will include residential blocks at the Allotments site, a supermarket, and new commercial and institutional buildings at the NWO site.

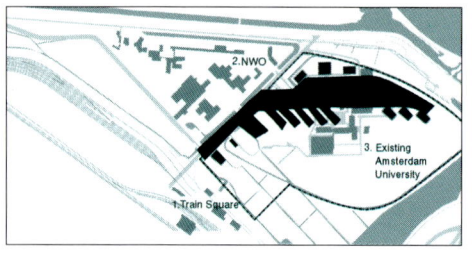

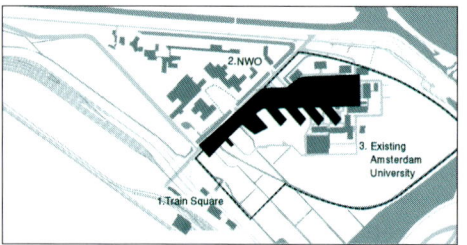

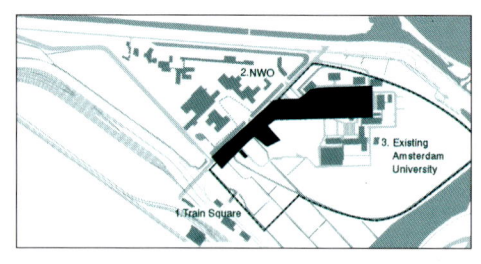

Flexibility (for expansion and contraction)

The design is flexible for expansion and contraction of floor space.

The building configuration enables the department buildings (i.e. the "fingers") to be built independently and incrementally according to the Client's requirements and cash flow.

The department floor plates are based on standard modules of 21.6m x 57m, which is adaptable for both laboratory and offices on a single floor. As the service cores are located outside the main floor plate, the overall efficiency achievable for each "finger" is high @ 83%.

The "fingers" may be extended, should additional floor areas be required.

In the event of surplus space, the departmental blocks as modular steel-constructed plug-ins may be leased out or dismantled, without affecting the overall functioning of the building complex.

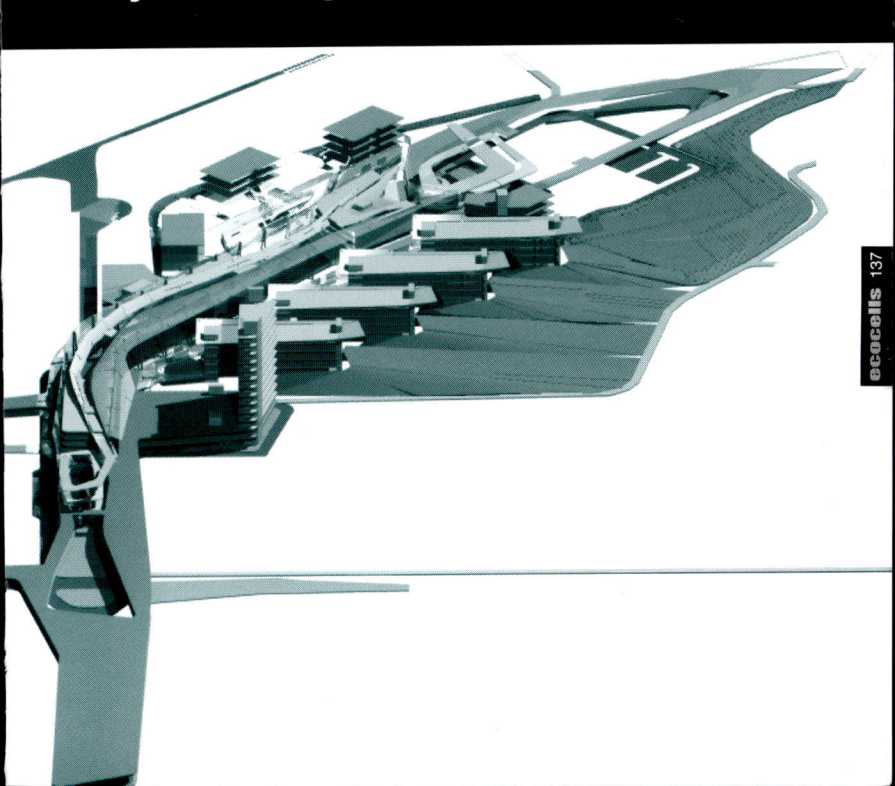

4. Design as Eco-mimesis
by Ken Yeang

- The host organism

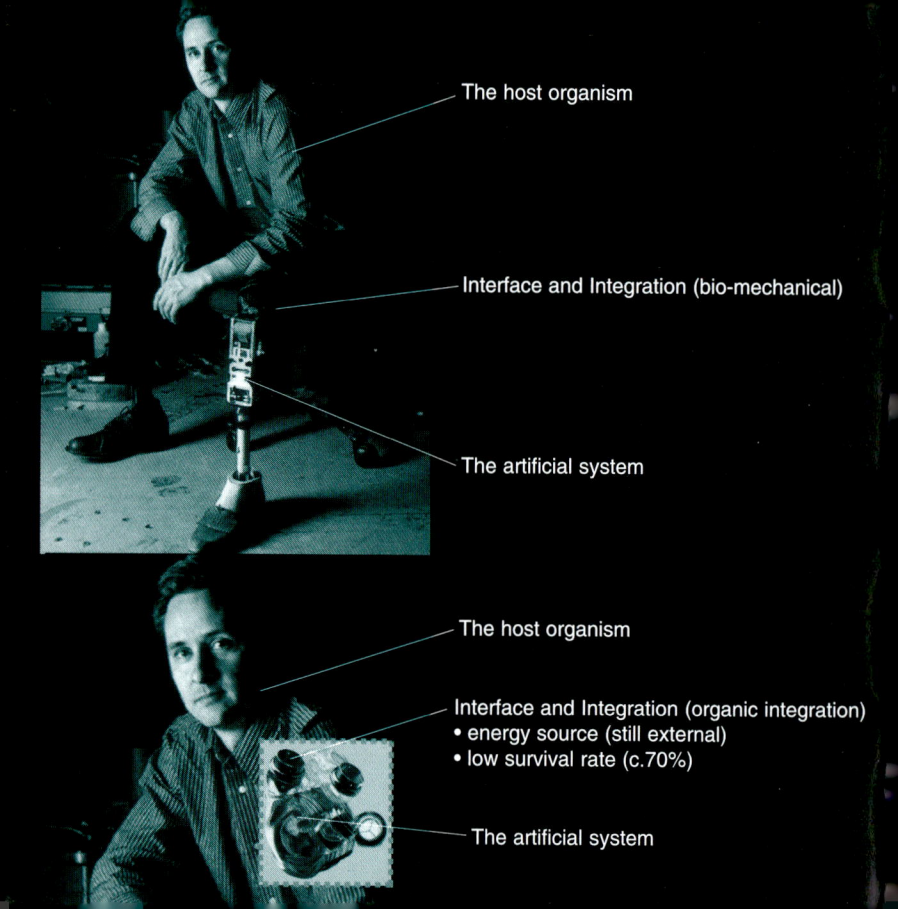

- Interface and Integration (bio-mechanical)

- The artificial system

- The host organism

- Interface and Integration (organic integration)
  • energy source (still external)
  • low survival rate (c.70%)

- The artificial system

Design as Eco-mimesis

I see the shelters that we build as essentially an extension of our clothing. A shelter provides us with another layer of enclosure between ourselves and the natural environment that is the biosphere. It offers us protection from the climate outside, besides fulfilling other human functions such as provision of security, privacy and other symbolic, aesthetic and cultural aspects.

Shelter is an enclosure that serves fundamentally as an environmental filter, that moderates between the climate at the outside natural environment with some man-generated activity on the inside (whether it is for residential, commercial, entertainment, industrial or simply for storage use) at some level of comfort or some required level of internal environmental conditions.

The outside environment is subject to the vicissitudes of the climatic elements. The extent of protection from these in our shelters varies depending on the biome or the climatic zone and latitude in which our shelter is located. For instance, our shelter may be in the cold climatic zone located in the upper parts of the hemisphere, or in the temperate climatic zone or in the hot-humid tropics. The extent of shelter and level of environmental filtering of the outside meteorological factors (sun, wind, rain, snow, etc.) and dependent on the outside climate and the activity within that shelter. An enclosure is often insufficient to provide the expected internal comfort conditions. We may need to supplement these by some mechanical and electrical environmental-conditioning system (whether by heating or cooling or ventilating, etc.) to ensure a level of comfort for humans to carry out their activities.

However, man can build shelters and artificial structures in huge aggregations as cities and at such significant scales that far exceed the capabilities of any other species in nature. The building of shelters and the construction of other components of the man-made environment such as roads and paved surfaces have a significant impact on our biosphere and on its natural resources. Many of these resources used by humankind are non-renewable and are rapidly depleting.

Building debris constitute 26 percent of the waste discarded into landfills. Buildings use up to 45 percent of the total consumption of non-renewable energy. Those involved in the creating and the production of buildings have certainly great responsibilities with regard to ensuring the sustainable future of our life on earth.

Shelters use huge amounts of energy in the production of building materials, and also large amounts of energy and materials in their operations. They also discharge huge amounts of energy and waste materials and pollutants into the natural environment.

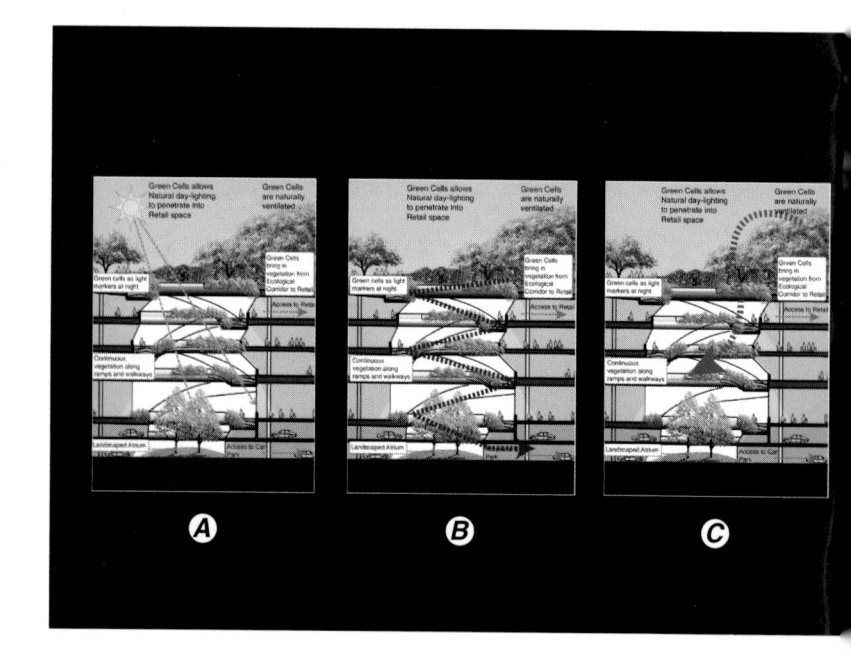

The earth's natural systems have thresholds and can assimilate only so much of these outputs and destructive actions beyond which irreparable damage can be done.

The natural environment also consists of both abiotic and biotic constituents, both acting together as a whole to form ecosystems. Yet significantly most of our shelters are essentially inorganic. By building more and more of these shelters to accommodate our increasing population, we are in effect making the world more and more inorganic and artificial, with a concurrent loss of biodiversity.

A Sun

B Rainwater collection & recycling

C Vegetation

D Natural ventilation

E Sewerage recycling tanks

What we need to do is to balance the present inorganicness of our man-made environment with more organic mass in our shelters. We need to literally green them with as much landscaping as possible and to systemically integrate vegetation and biomassinto our buildings. This will not only balance the extensively abiotic constituents of our current man-made environment, it will encourage an increase in ecosystem biodiversity as well as reduce the heat-island effect on our cities.

There are of course other aspects of human shelter than just their ecological consequences. Shelters provide homes for our families. They provide the social, physical, economic, emotional justification of our existence. They give joy to people in their lives. Grand civic shelters remind us of our humanity and identity. Shelters gives pleasure in enabling our myriad activities to be carried out under protection from the inclement weather. They provide us with comfort and an improved standard of living. Of course 15-19 percent of humans is still shelterless, and this right for shelter is a prerequisite for all of humanity.

Those responsible for the production of our shelters have a longer term responsibility beyond their provision. We must ask what happens to these shelters at the end of their useful life? In the long term, we must ensure that the materials that make up our shelters are reused, recycled and eventually reintegrated into the biosphere. We should be responsible for our shelters from source-to-sink.

By analogy, a building is like a prosthesis, like an artificial arm that, in order to function well, must be integral with the human body as its organic host system. Buildings are essentially artificial man-made systems that must be similarly integral with the biosphere's ecosystems as the equivalent organic host for our man-made shelters. It is this interface that many if not most of our man-made built environments or shelters have failed to integrate effectively.

It is with regard to this aspect that the two projects presented here are part of our endeavours by design to achieve this systemic integration with nature in as seamlessly a relationship as possible. For a sustainable future, our shelters must become a whole again with nature.

Dr. Ken Yeang